Supporting Windows 8.1 Exam 70-688

Lab Manual

Patrick Regan

WILEY

EXECUTIVE EDITOR	John Kane
EDITORIAL ASSISTANT	Jessy Lentz
EXECUTIVE MARKETING MANAGER	Chris Ruel
SENIOR PRODUCTION & MANUFACTURING MANAGER	Janis Soo
ASSOCIATE PRODUCTION MANAGER	Joyce Poh

www.wiley.com/college/microsoft or
call the MOAC Toll-Free Number: 888-764-7001 (U.S. & Canada only)

ISBN 978-1-118-88255-9

Printed in the United States of America

BRIEF CONTENTS

CONTENTS

LAB 1
SUPPORTING AN OPERATING SYSTEM INSTALLATION

THIS LAB CONTAINS THE FOLLOWING EXERCISES AND ACTIVITIES:

Exercise 1.1 Creating a VHD Boot File Using Disk Management

Exercise 1.2 Creating a VHD Boot File Using DiskPart and DISM

Exercise 1.3 Adding the VHD Image to the Boot Menu

Exercise 1.4 Updating a Windows Image

Lab Challenge Using Windows To Go

BEFORE YOU BEGIN

The lab environment consists of student workstations connected to a local area network, along with a server that functions as the domain controller for a domain called contoso.com. The computers required for this lab are listed in Table 1-1.

Table 1-1
Computers required for Lab 1

Computer	Operating System	Computer Name
Server	Windows Server 2012 R2	RWDC01
Server	Windows Server 2012 R2	Server02
Client	Windows 8.1	Win8A

In addition to the computers, you will also need the software listed in Table 1-2 to complete Lab 1.

Table 1-2
Software required for Lab 1

Software	Location
Update for Internet Explorer 11 for Windows 8.1 for x64-based systems (KB2901549) (Windows8.1-KB2901549-x64.msu)	\\rwdc01\software
Lab 1 student worksheet	Lab01_worksheet.docx (provided by instructor)

Working with Lab Worksheets

Each lab in this manual requires that you answer questions, shoot screen shots, and perform other activities that you will document in a worksheet named for the lab, such as Lab01_worksheet.docx. You will find these worksheets on the book companion site. It is recommended that you use a USB flash drive to store your worksheets, so you can submit them to your instructor for review. As you perform the exercises in each lab, open the appropriate worksheet file, fill in the required information, and then save the file to your flash drive.

SCENARIO

After completing this lab, you will be able to:

■ Create a VHD Boot File Using Disk Management

■ Create a VHD Boot File Using Disk PART and DISM

■ Add the VHD Image to the Boot Menu

■ Manage Desktop Images

■ Using Windows To Go

Estimated lab time: 90 minutes

Exercise 1.1	Creating a VHD Boot File Using Disk Management
Overview	In this exercise, you will create a VHD Boot file using Disk Management.
Mindset	A native VHD boot file allows you to mount and boot from the operating system contained within the VHD, which allows you to test the performance and compatibility on your current system. It can also be used to streamline image management.
Completion time	15 minutes

1. On *Win8A*, log on using the **contoso\administrator** account and the **Pa$$w0rd** password.

2. Click the **Desktop** tile.

3. Right-click the **Start** button and, from the context menu that appears, choose **Computer Management**. The *Computer Management* console opens.

4. Under *Storage*, click **Disk Management** (see Figure 1-1). Then click the **Action** menu and choose **Create VHD**.

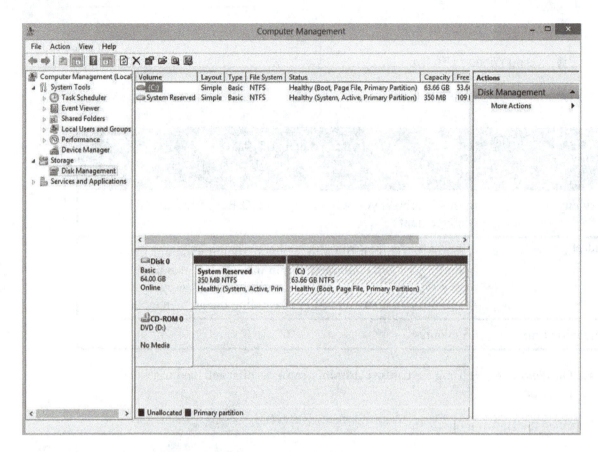

Figure 1-1
Computer Management console's Disk Management node

Question 1	What type of infrastructure allows you to have users access centrally managed desktops using RPD?

5. In the *Location* text box, type **C:\Win8VHDA**. For the *Virtual hard disk size* setting, specify **20** GB. For the *Virtual hard disk type* setting, select **Dynamically expanding**.

6. Take a screen shot of the *Create and Attach Virtual Hard Disk* dialog box by pressing **Alt+PrtScr** and then paste it into your Lab 1 worksheet file in the page provided by pressing **Ctrl+V**.

7. Click **OK** to close the *Create and Attach Virtual Hard Disk* dialog box.

8. Right-click **Disk 1** and choose **Initialize Disk**.

9. In the *Initialize Disk* dialog box, click **OK**.

10. Right-click the **Disk 1 Unallocated** disk space and choose **New Simple Volume**.

11. In the *Welcome to the New Simple Volume* Wizard, click **Next**.

12. On the *Specify Volume Size* page, click **Next**.

13. On the *Assign Drive Letter or Path* page, answer the following question and then click **Next**.

Question 2	*What drive letter will be assigned to the drive?*

14. On the *Format Partition* page, click **Next**.

15. When the wizard is complete, click **Finish**.

16. If a dialog box is open, prompting you to format a disk, click **Cancel** to close the dialog box. (You may see this dialog box in Step 19, below.)

17. To detach the VHD file, right-click **Disk 1** and choose **Detach VHD**. On the *Detach Virtual Hard Disk* dialog box, click **OK**.

18. To reattach the VHD file, click **Action > Attach VHD**.

19. Click the **Browse** button to browse to the *c:\Win8VHDA.vhd* file and then click **Open**. In the *Attach Virtual Hard Disk* dialog box, click **OK**.

End of exercise. Close Computer Management, but leave the computer logged into for the next exercise.

Exercise 1.2	Creating a VHD Boot File Using DiskPart and DISM
Overview	In this exercise, you will create a VHD Boot file using command prompt utilities.
Mindset	DiskPart allows you to manage disk partitions, including partitioning, formatting, deleting, shrinking, and assigning drive letters; you also can change drive letters. DISM allows you to manage offline Windows images.
Completion time	25 minutes

1. On *Win8A*, right-click the **Start** button and choose **Command Prompt** (**Admin**).

2. At the command prompt, execute the following command:

```
diskpart
```

Question 3	*How would you describe the DiskPart command that allows you to execute subcommands?*

3. To create a VHD file, execute the following commands at the command prompt (see Figure 1-2):

```
create vdisk file=c:\Win8VHDB.vhd maximum=20512
type=expandable

select vdisk file=c:\Win8VHDB.vhd

attach vdisk
```

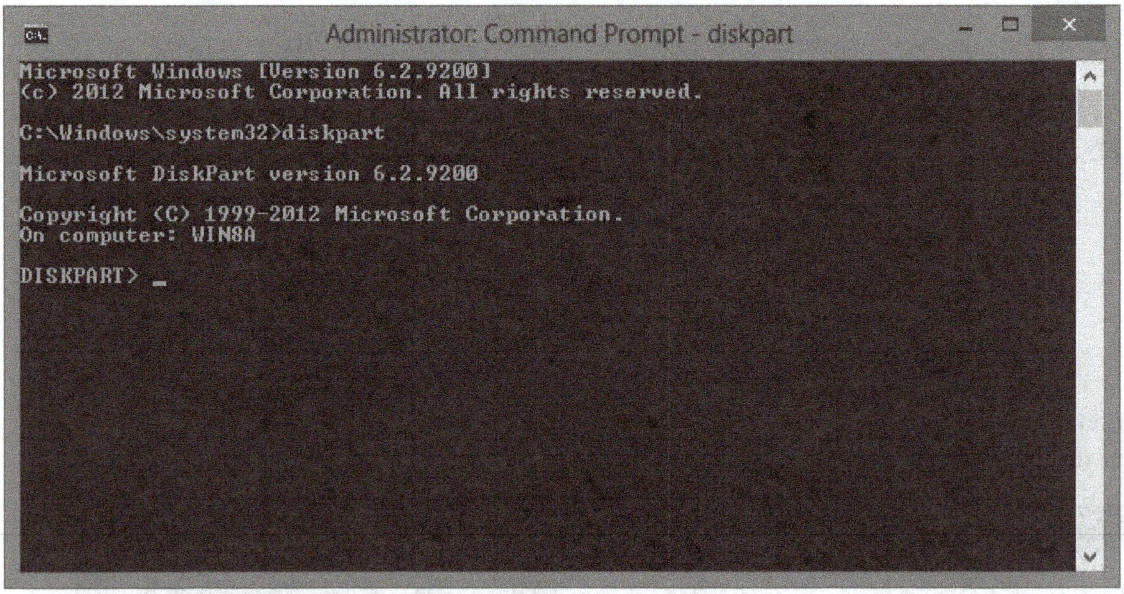

Figure 1-2
The DISKPART command prompt

4. Take a screen shot of the command prompt window by pressing **Alt+PrtScr** and then paste it into your Lab 1 worksheet file in the page provided by pressing **Ctrl+V**.

5. Execute the following command to create the partition, assign the F drive letter, and then format the disk:

```
create partition primary

assign letter=f

format quick
```

6. To exit DiskPart, execute the following command:

```
exit
```

7. If any dialog boxes are open, prompting you to format a disk, click **Cancel** to close the dialog box.

8. To apply the Windows image (install.wim) to the *F* drive, execute the following commands:

```
Dism /apply-image /imagefile:\\rwdc01\software\install.wim
/index:1 /ApplyDir:F:\
```

9. Open *File Explorer* by clicking the **File Explorer** icon on the taskbar.

10. Navigate to the *F* drive to see the standard Windows folders.

11. Take a screen shot of the *File Explorer* window by pressing **Alt+PrtScr** and then paste it into your Lab 1 worksheet file in the page provided by pressing **Ctrl+V**.

End of exercise. Leave the command prompt window open for the next exercise.

Exercise 1.3	Adding the VHD Image to the Boot Menu
Overview	In this exercise, you will add the VHD image to the boot menu that you created in the last exercise using the BCD Editor.
Mindset	BCD Editor (bcdedit.exe) is used to modify the boot menu that appears before the Windows operating system is loaded.
Completion time	15 minutes

1. On *Win8A*, to view the current BCD store, execute the following command (as shown in Figure 1-3):

```
bcdedit /enum
```

Question 4	*What is the GUID for the current boot volume?*

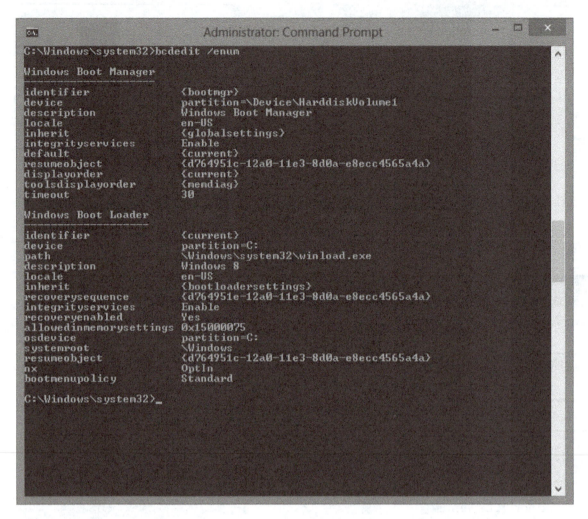

Figure 1-3
The BCD store

2. To copy the boot volume, execute the following commands at the command prompt:

```
bcdedit /copy {default} /d "Windows 8 VHD Boot"
```

Question 5	What is the GUID for the new boot volume?

3. To add the VHD image to the boot menu, execute the following commands at the command prompt:

```
bcdedit /set {GUID} device vhd=[c:]\win8vhdb.vhd
```

```
bcdedit /set {GUID} osdevice vhd=[c:]\win8vhdb.vhd
```

```
bcdedit /set {GUID} detecthal on
```

whereby *{GUID}* is a long string with braces as recorded in Question 5. Be sure to include the braces when typing the commands.

4. Maximize the command prompt window by clicking the maximize button (second button) of the top-left corner of the command prompt window.

5. To view the current BCD store, execute the following command:

```
bcdedit /enum
```

6. Take a screen shot of the command prompt window by pressing **Alt+PrtScr** and then paste it into your Lab 1 worksheet file in the page provided by pressing **Ctrl+V**.

7. Reboot the computer. Notice the two options on the *Choose an operating system* screen. Boot to Windows 8.1.

End of exercise. Leave the computer running for the next exercise.

Exercise 1.4	Updating a Windows Image
Overview	From time to time, you need to patch a Windows image. In this exercise, you will add a Windows update package to the install.wim file.
Mindset	When you update an installation image using the Dism command, the Windows package must be a cabinet (.cab) file or a Windows Update Stand-alone Installation (.msu) file.
Completion time	20 minutes

1. On *Win8A*, log on using the **contoso\administrator** account and the **Pa$$w0rd** password. Click the **Desktop** tile.

2. On *Win8A*, click the **File Explorer** icon, then create a **C:\Package** folder.

3. Create a **C:\Offline** folder.

4. Create a **C:\Image** folder.

5. Open the **\\rwdc01\software** folder.

6. Copy the *Windows8.1-KB2901549-x64.msu* file and the *install.wim* file to the *C:\Package* folder.

7. Right-click the **Start** button and choose **Command Prompt (Admin)**.

8. To change to the *C:\Software* folder, execute the following command at the command prompt:

```
cd\Package
```

9. To extract the cab files from the *Windows8.1-KB2901549-x64.msu* file, execute the following command:

   ```
   Windows8.1-KB2901549-x64.msu /extract:C:\Package
   ```

10. Using File Explorer, view the content of the *C:\Package* folder.

11. Take a screen shot of the *Package* folder by pressing **Alt+Prt Scr** and then paste it into your Lab 1 worksheet file in the page provided by pressing **Ctrl+V**.

12. From the *\\rwdc01\software* folder, copy the **install.wim** file to the *C:\Image* folder.

Question 6	What is the first step that you have to perform before you can add a Windows package to a WIM file?

13. In the *Administrator: Command Prompt* window, to mount the *c:\Software\install.wim* file, execute the following command:

    ```
    dism /Mount-Wim /WimFile:C:\Image\install.wim /index:1
    /MountDir:C:\Offline
    ```

14. To get information about the WIM file, execute the following command:

    ```
    dism /Get-WimInfo /WimFile:C:\Image\install.wim /index:1
    ```

15. To add the package to the WIM image, execute the following command:

    ```
    dism /image:C:\Offline /Add-Package
    /Packagepath:C:\Package\Windows8.1-KB2901549-x64.cab
    ```

16. To commit the changes to the WIM file, execute the following command:

    ```
    dism /Commit-Wim /MountDir:C:\Offline
    ```

17. Assuming that this is an image of Windows PE, open the **C:\Offline\Windows\System32** folder.

18. Click **View > File name extensions**.

19. Click the **Home** menu and then click **New > Text Document**.

20. Change the filename to **startnet.cmd**. Make sure that the .txt filename extension is changed to .cmd. When you are prompted to confirm that you want to rename the file name extension, click **Yes**.

21. Right-click **Startet.cmd** file and choose **Edit**.

22. When *Notepad* opens, type **wpeinit**.

23. Click **File > Exit**. When you are prompted to save the changes, click **Save**.

24. To dismount the WIM file, execute the following command at the command prompt window:

```
dism /Unmount-Wim /MountDir:C:\Offline /commit
```

25. Take a screen shot of the *Command Prompt* by pressing **Alt+Prt Scr** and then paste it into your Lab 1 worksheet file in the page provided by pressing **Ctrl+V**.

26. Close the *Administrator: Command Prompt* window.

End of exercise. Close all windows.

Lab Challenge	Using Windows To Go
Overview	To complete this challenge, you must complete a written exercise that demonstrates how to use Windows to Go.
Mindset	You are an administrator for the Contoso Corporation. You have an application that a manager must run on his Windows tablet, but you want the application installed on a server and you want the application to be isolated from other applications. You decide to use Windows To Go in order to accomplish these goals. This is a written exercise only. To review how to use Windows To Go, refer to Lesson 1 of the MOAC 70-688 textbook.
Completion time	15 minutes

Write the steps you would use to set up Windows to Go workspace.

End of lab.

LAB 2
SUPPORTING DESKTOP APPLICATIONS

THIS LAB CONTAINS THE FOLLOWING EXERCISES AND ACTIVITIES:

Exercise 2.1   Installing and Using the Application Compatibility Tool (ACT) Kit

Exercise 2.2   Installing Applications

Exercise 2.3   Using Remote Applications

Exercise 2.4   Using App-V Programs

Lab Challenge   Deploying the App-V Program

BEFORE YOU BEGIN

The lab environment consists of student workstations connected to a local area network, along with a server that functions as the domain controller for a domain called contoso.com. The computers required for this lab are listed in Table 2-1.

Table 2-1
Computers Required for Lab 2

Computer	Operating System	Computer Name
Server	Windows Server 2012 R2	RWDC01
Server	Windows Server 2012 R2	Server02
Client	Windows 8.1	Win8A
Client	Windows 8.1	Win8B

In addition to the computers, you will also need the software listed in Table 2-2 to complete Lab 2.

Table 2-2
Software Required for Lab 2

Software	Location
Windows Assessment and Deployment Kit for Windows Server 8.1	\\rwdc01\software
Desktop Optimization Pack 2013 R2	\\rwdc01\software
PowerPoint Viewer (PowerPointViewer.exe)	\\rwdc01\software
Test PowerPoint presentation	\\rwdc01\software
Assessment and Deployment Kit for Windows 8.1	\\rwdc01\software
Lab 2 student worksheet	Lab02_worksheet.docx (provided by instructor)

Working with Lab Worksheets

Each lab in this manual requires that you answer questions, shoot screen shots, and perform other activities that you will document in a worksheet named for the lab, such as Lab02_worksheet.docx. You will find these worksheets on the book companion site. It is recommended that you use a USB flash drive to store your worksheets so you can submit them to your instructor for review. As you perform the exercises in each lab, open the appropriate worksheet file, fill in the required information, and then save the file to your flash drive.

SCENARIO

After completing this lab, you will be able to:

- Install and use the Application Compatibility Tool (ACT) Kit

- Assign an application using a GPO

- Install and configure remote applications

- Create and deploy an App-V Program

Estimated lab time: 150 minutes

Exercise 2.1	Installing and Using Application Compatibility Tool (ACT) Kit
Overview	In this exercise, you will install SQL Express and then install the Application Compatibility Toolkit.
Mindset	The Application Compatibility Toolkit (ACT) helps determine whether applications, devices, and computers within your organization can run with newer versions of Windows.
Completion time	35 minutes

1. On *Server02*, log on using the **contoso\administrator** account and the **Pa$$w0rd** password.

2. On *Server02*, open **File Explorer**, open the **\\rwdc01\software\Windows Kits\8.1\ADK** folder, and then double-click **adksetup**. If you are prompted to confirm that you want to run the file, click **Run**.

3. On the *Specify Location* page, click **Next**.

4. On the *Join the Customer Experience Improvement Program (CEIP)* page, click **Next**.

5. On the *License Agreement* page, click **Accept**.

6. On the *Select the features you want to install* page, deselect all features except **Application Compatibility Toolkit (ACT)** and **Microsoft SQL Server 2012 Express**. Click **Install**.

7. Take a screen shot of the *Welcome to the Windows Assessment and Deployment Kit for Windows Server 8.1* screen by pressing **Alt+PrtScr** and then paste it into your Lab 2 worksheet file in the page provided by pressing **Ctrl+V**.

8. Click **Close**.

9. Click the **Start** menu. Then, on the Start screen, type **acm**. From the *Results* list, click **Application Compatibility Manager**. The *Application Compatibility Manager* opens.

10. In the *Welcome to the ACT Configuration* Wizard, click **Next**.

11. On the *Do you want to use this computer to run an ACT Log Processing Service?* page, Click **Next**.

12. On the Configure Your ACT Database Settings page, for the *SQL Server* setting, select **(local)\ADK** and then click **Connect**.

13. In the *Database:* text box, type **ACT** and then click **Next**. On the *Configure Your ACT Database Settings* page, click **Next**.

14. On the *Configure Your Log File Location* dialog box, click **Browse**.

15. In the *Browse for Folder* dialog box, expand **This PC**, and then click **Local Disk (C:)**. Click **Make New Folder** and then create a folder called **Logs**. With *Logs* highlighted, click **OK**.

16. Back on the *Configure Your Log File Location* page, click **Next**.

17. On the *Configure Your ACT Log Processing Service Account* page, click **Next**.

18. On the *Congratulations* page, click **Finish**.

19. In the left pane of the *Application Compatibility Manager* window, click **Collect**.

20. On the menu at the top of the screen, click **File > New**.

21. On the *Choose the type of package to create* page, click **Inventory collection package**.

22. Take a screen shot of the *Set up your inventory package* window by pressing **Alt+PrtScr** and then paste it into your Lab 2 worksheet file in the page provided by pressing **Ctrl+V**.

23. Click **Create**.

24. In the *Save Data Collection Package* dialog box, answer the following question.

Question 1	Where will the package be saved?

25. In the *File name* text box, type **\\rwdc01\software**. Click **Save**, and then click **Save** again.

Question 2	What are the next steps for your inventory collection package?

26. Click **Finish**.

27. Close **Collect - Microsoft Application Compatibility Manager**.

28. Click the **Start** button. When the *Start* page opens, click the **Apps** down arrow button. Then in the *Windows Kits* section, click **Compatibility Administrator (64-bit)**.

    Please note that you will need to scroll over to see the Windows Kits section and you will have to hover the mouse over the applications to find the Compatibility Administrator (64-bit) tile.

29. When *Compatibility Administrator (64-bit)* opens, under the *System Database (64-bit)* mode, expand **Applications**, and then click **Adobe Photoshop CS4 (64 Bit)**.

Question 3	How many fixes are available for Adobe Photoshop CS4 (64 Bit)

Question 4	Which Compatibility Modes setting is available for Photoshop?

End of exercise. Close Compatibility Administrator (64-bit) but remain logged into the computer for the next exercise.

Exercise 2.2	Installing Applications
Overview	During this exercise, you will perform a software installation of an MSI file using group policies. MSI applications can be used to install applications and upgrade existing applications.
Mindset	After you create an application with ACT, you must deploy the application to the client. One method to deploy applications is to use Group Policy.
Completion time	10 minutes

1. On *RWDC01*, log on using the **contoso\administrator** account and the **Pa$$w0rd** password. The *Server Manager* console opens.

2. Using *Server Manager*, under the *Tools* section, click **Group Policy Management**.

3. On the *Group Policy Management* console, expand **Forest: CONTOSO.COM** and then expand **Domains**.

4. Right-click **contoso.com** and choose **Create a GPO in this domain, and Link it here**.

5. In the *New GPO* dialog box, in the *Name* text box, type **Software Install** and then click **OK**.

6. Expand the **CONTOSO.COM** node.

7. Right-click the **Software Install** node and choose **Edit**. The *Group Policy Management Editor* opens (see Figure 2-1).

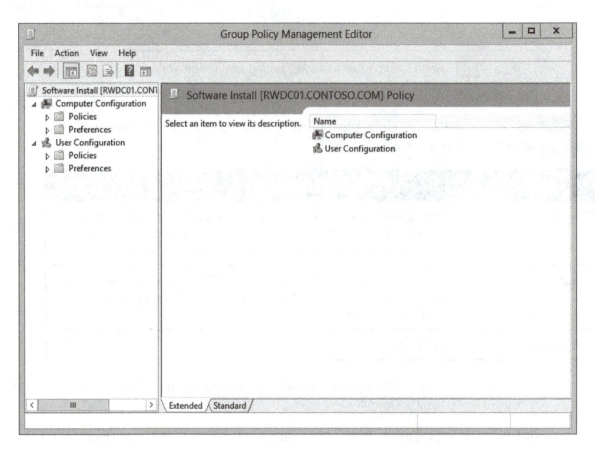

Figure 2-1
The Group Policy Management Editor

8. Navigate to and click **Computer Configuration\Policies\Software Settings**.

9. Right-click the **Software installation** and choose **New > Package**. The *Open* dialog box appears.

10. Navigate to **\\RWDC01\Software**. Click **New_Package1** and then click **Open**.

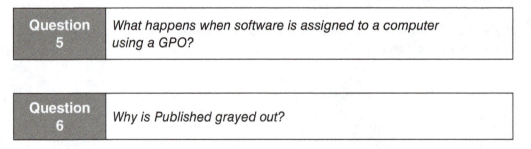

Question 5	What happens when software is assigned to a computer using a GPO?

Question 6	Why is Published grayed out?

11. In the *Deploy Software* dialog box, click **Assigned** and then click **OK**. If you get an error with the MMC, select **Continue running and ignore errors with this snap-in for the rest of the session**, and then click **OK**. The *Microsoft ACT 6.0 Inventory Collection package* appears in the right pane.

12. Take a screen shot of the *Group Policy Management Editor* showing the *Software installation* node by pressing **Alt+PrtScr** and then paste it into your Lab 2 worksheet file in the page provided by pressing **Ctrl+V**.

End of exercise. On *RWDC01*, close the Group Policy Management Editor and then close the Group Policy Management console. On *Server02*, close Microsoft Application Compatibility Manager. Leave the computer logged on for the next exercise.

Exercise 2.3	Using Remote Applications
Overview	In this exercise, you will use the RemoteApp feature to access and run an application on a remote server.
Mindset	To make an application available to users without actually installing the application on each client computer, users can run the application using the RemoteApp feature.
Completion time	50 minutes

First, you'll need to install PowerPoint Viewer by performing the following steps:

1. On *Server02*, click the **File Explorer** button on the taskbar to open *File Explorer*.

2. Using *File Explorer*, open the **\\rwdc01\software** folder.

3. Double-click the **PowerPointViewer.exe** installation file. If a security warning prompts you to confirm that you want to run this file, click **Run**.

4. On the *Microsoft Software License Terms* page, select **Click here to accept the Microsoft Software License Terms** and then click **Continue**.

5. On the *Microsoft PowerPoint Viewer* Wizard page, click **Next**.

6. When you are prompted to confirm where to install the viewer, click **Install**.

7. When the installation is complete, click **OK**.

Next, install Remote Desktop Services by performing the following steps:

1. Reboot **Server02**, log on using the **contoso\administrator** account and the **Pa$$w0rd** password.

2. On *Server02*, open **Server Manager** if it is not open already, and then click **Manage > Add Roles and Features**.

3. On the *Add Roles and Features* Wizard page, click **Next**.

4. On the *Select installation type* page, click **Remote Desktop Services Installation** (see Figure 2-2) and then click **Next**.

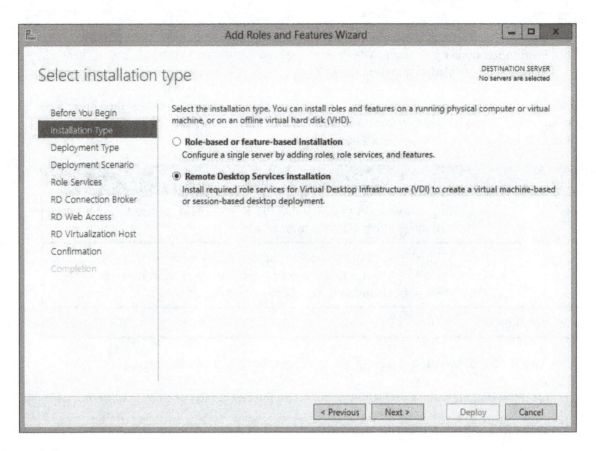

Figure 2-2
Specifying the Remote Desktop Services Installation option

5. On the *Select deployment type* page, click **Standard deployment** and then click **Next**.

6. On the *Select deployment scenario* page, click **Session-based desktop deployment** and then click **Next**.

7. On the *Review role services* page, click **Next**.

8. On the *Specify RD Connection Broker server* page, with **Server02.contoso.com** highlighted, click the **>** arrow button and then click **Next**.

9. On the *Specify RD Web Access server* page, with **Server02.contoso.com** highlighted, click the **>** arrow button and then click **Next**.

10. On the *Specify RD Session Host servers* page, with **Server02.contoso.com** highlighted, click the **>** arrow button and then click **Next**.

11. On the *Confirm selections* page, select **Restart the destination server automatically if required** and then click **Deploy**.

12. After *Server02* reboots, log on to **Server02** using the **contoso\administrator** account and the **Pa$$w0rd** password. When *Server Manager* opens, the RD services will finish installing. If you get a *Remote Desktop licensing mode is not configured* popup, you can click the **x** button to close the popup.

Question 7	When Server Manager starts, how many days are available to use the Remote Desktop licensing mode?

13. Shortly after you log on, the *View progress* window opens. When *Remote Desktop Services role services* is installed, click **Close** to close the *Add Roles and Features Wizard* dialog box.

14. Using *Server Manager*, under the Dashboard on the left, click **Remote Desktop Services**.

15. On the *Overview* page, in the left column, click **Collections**.

16. In the *Collections* section, click **Tasks > Create Session Collection**. You may need to scroll over to see the *Tasks* option, as shown in Figure 2-3.

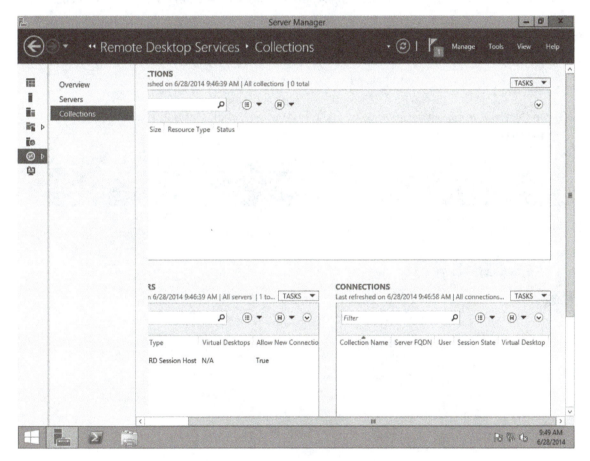

Figure 2-3
Showing the Tasks option

17. On the *Create Collection* Wizard page, click **Next**.

18. On the *Name the collection* page, in the *Name* text box, type **Server02** and then click **Next**.

19. On the *Specify RD Session Host servers* page, with **Server02.contoso.com** highlighted, click the **>** arrow button and then click **Next**.

20. On the *Specify user groups* page, *CONTOSO\Domain Users* is already added. Click **Next**.

21. On the *Specify user profile disks* page, in the *Location of user profile disks* text box, type **C:\UserProfile** and then click **Next**.

22. On the *Confirm selections* page, click **Create**.

23. When the collection is created, click **Close**.

24. Press **Ctrl+PrtScr** to take a screen shot of the *Collections* page. Press **Ctrl+V** to paste the image on the page provided in the Lab 2 worksheet file.

Next, you'll need to configure RemoteApp Applications by performing the following steps:

1. On *Server02*, using *Server Manager*, click **Remote Desktop Services** at the top of the Server Manager window.

2. Under *Collections*, click **Server02**.

3. In the *RemoteApp Programs* section (see Figure 2-4), click **Publish RemoteApp programs**.

Figure 2-4
Accessing the RemoteApp Programs section

4. In the *Publish RemoteApp Programs* dialog box, click **Add**.

5. In the *Open* dialog box, double-click the **Program Files (x86)** folder, double-click **Microsoft Office** folder, double-click the **Office14**, and then click **PPTView**.

6. Answer the following question and then click **Open**.

Question 8	*What was the full path to the PPTView?*

7. Back on the *Select RemoteApp programs* page, click **Next**.

8. On the *Confirmation* page, click **Publish**.

9. Click **Close** to close the *Publish RemoteApp Programs* window.

10. Press **Ctrl+PrtScr** to take a screen shot of the *Server02* collection showing the *RemoteApp Programs* section. Press **Ctrl+V** to paste the image on the page provided in the Lab 2 worksheet file.

11. Click the **Start** button, and then click **Administrative Tools**.

12. When the *Administrative Tools* folder opens, double-click **Internet Information Services (IIS) Manager**.

13. In *Internet Information Services (IIS) Manager*, expand **SERVER02**, and then click **Application Pools**. If you are prompted to confirm that you want to stay connected with the latest Web Platform Components, click **No**.

14. Right-click **RDWebAccess** and choose **Advanced Settings**.

15. If the *Identity* is configured to *ApplicationPoolIdentity*, click **ApplicationPoolIdentity**, and then click the . . . button. In the *Application Pool Identity* dialog box, change the *Built-in* account from *Application Pool Identity* to **NetworkService**. Click **OK** to close the *Application Pool Identity* dialog box.

16. Click **OK** to close the *Advanced Settings* dialog box.

17. Right-click **SERVER02** and choose **Stop**. Then right-click **SERVER02** and choose **Start**.

18. Close **Internet Information Services Manager**.

Next, you will use a RemoteApp application by performing the following steps:

1. On *Win8A*, log on using the **contoso\administrator** account and the **Pa$$w0rd** password.

2. Click the **Desktop** tile.

3. Open *Internet Explorer* by clicking the **Internet Explorer** icon on the taskbar and then go to the **https://server02.contoso.com/rdweb** website.

4. When a message indicates there is a problem with the website's security certificate, click **Continue to this website (not recommended)**.

5. At the bottom of the IE window, when you are prompted to run the *Microsoft Remote Desktop Services Web Access Control*, click **Allow**.

6. Click the **Certificate error** on the top of the IE window and then click **View certificates**.

7. In the *Certificate* dialog box, click **InstallCertificate**.

8. On the *Certificate Import* Wizard page, click **Local Machine** and then click **Next**.

9. On the *Certificate Store* page, click **Place all certificates in the following store**.

10. Click the **Browse** button. In the *Select Certificate Store* dialog box, click **Trusted Root Certification Authorities**, and then click **OK**.

11. Back on the *Certificate Store* page, click **Next**.

12. When the wizard finishes, click **Finish**.

13. When *The import was successful* message appears, click **OK**.

14. Click **OK** to close the *Certificate* dialog box.

15. On the *RemoteApp and Desktop Connection* window, log on as **contoso\administrator** using the **Pa$$w0rd** password.

16. Press **Ctrl+PrtScr** to take a screen shot of the *RemoteApp and Desktops* page showing the *PPTVIEW* icon. Press **Ctrl+V** to paste the image on the page provided in the Lab 2 worksheet file.

17. Double-click **PPTVIEW**.

18. In the *RemoteApp* dialog box, click **Connect**.

Question 9	*Where is the PowerPoint Viewer actually being executed?*

19. In the *Microsoft PowerPoint Viewer* dialog box, in the *File name* text box, type **\\rwdc01\software** and then click **Open**. Double-click **Test PowerPoint Presentation** and then click **Open**.

20. Press **Ctrl+PrtScr** to take a screen shot of the *Test PowerPoint Presentation* window. Press **Ctrl+V** to paste the image on the page provided in the Lab 2 worksheet file.

21. Close **PowerPoint Viewer** and then close the **Test PowerPoint Presentation** window.

22. Close **Internet Explorer**.

End of exercise. Log off of Server02 and Win8A.

Exercise 2.4	Using App-V Programs
Overview	In this exercise, you will create an App-V program and then you will deploy it.
Mindset	App-V allows you to run virtual applications, which are applications that run in an isolated environment on a computer.
Completion time	40 minutes

First, you will install the App-V 5.0 client by performing the following steps:

1. Log on to *Win8A* log on using the **contoso\administrator** account and the **Pa$$w0rd** password. Click the **Desktop** tile, then open *File Explorer* by clicking the **File Explorer** icon on the taskbar.

2. Using *File Explorer*, open the **\\rwdc01\software** folder.

3. Right-click the SW **DVD5 Dsktp Optimization Pck SA 2013 R2 English -2 MLF X18-90519** ISO and choose **Mount**.

4. In the *MDOP2013* window, double-click the **Launcher** folder and then double-click **launcher**.

5. On the *Microsoft Desktop Optimization Pack for Software Assurance 2013 R2* page, click **Application Virtualization for Desktops**.

6. Click **App-V 5.0 SP2 Client**.

7. On the *5.0 Client Setup* page, click **Install**.

8. On the *Software License Terms* page, click **I accept the license terms** and then click **Next**.

9. If you are prompted to use Microsoft Update, click **I don't want to use Microsoft Update** and then click **Next**.

10. On the *Customer Experience Improvement Program* page, click **Install**.

11. When the installation finishes, click **Restart later**.

Now you will install the App-V 5.0 sequencer by performing the following steps:

1. On the *Microsoft Application Virtualization for Desktops* menu, under the *App-V 5.0 SP2* category, click **App-V 5.0 SP2 Sequencer**.

2. Click **Install**.

3. Review the *Software Licenses Terms* screen, select **I accept the license terms**, and then click **Next**.

4. On the *Customer Experience Improvement Program* screen, click **Install** to accept the default.

5. When the message *Setup completed successfully* appears, take a screen shot by pressing **Alt+PrtScr** and then paste it into your Lab 2 worksheet file in the page provided by pressing **Ctrl+V**.

6. Click **Close**.

Next, you will sequence an application by performing the following steps:

1. Reboot **Win8A**.

2. On *Win8A*, log on using the **contoso\administrator** account and the **Pa$$w0rd** password.

3. Type **Windows Defender**, and then press **Enter**.

4. When *Windows Defender* starts, click the **Settings** tab.

5. Deselect the **Turn on real-time protection** option. Click **Save Changes**, and then click **Cancel**. When you are warned that this app has been turned off and isn't monitoring your computer, click **Close** (the white X button) in the upper-right corner.

6. Click the **Start** button, type **Sequencer**, and then press **Enter**.

7. In the *Microsoft Application Virtualization Sequencer* window (see Figure 2-5), click **Create a New Virtual Application Package**.

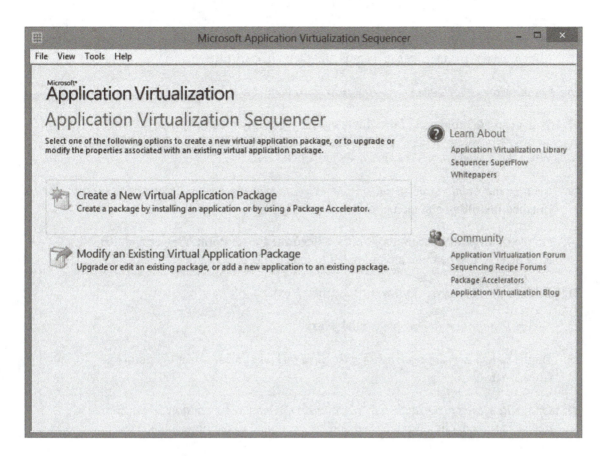

Figure 2-5
The Application Virtualization Sequencer

8. Accept the **Create Package (default)** setting by clicking **Next**.

9. On the *Prepare the computer for creating a virtual package* page, ensure there are no issues listed that need to be resolved. Because we disabled Windows Defender, real-time protection is turned off, so you can ignore the Windows Defender warning and then click **Next**.

10. On the *Type of Application* page, accept the **Standard Application (default)** setting by clicking **Next**.

11. On the *Select Installer* page, click **Browse** to navigate. When the *Select installation file* dialog box opens, in the *File name* text box, type **\\rwdc01\software** and then press **Enter**. Click the **PowerPointViewer.exe** file and then click **Open**.

12. Back on the *Select Installer* page, click **Next** to continue.

13. On the *Package Name* screen, in the *Virtual Application Package Name* field, type **PowerPoint Viewer**.

14. For the *Primary Virtual Application Directory (required)* field, type **c:\Program Files\PowerPoint Viewer**. Click **Next**.

15. When the *PowerPointViewer* installation program starts, click **Click here to accept the Microsoft Software License Terms** and then click **Continue**.

16. On the *Microsoft PowerPoint Viewer* Wizard page, click **Next**.

17. When you are prompted to install the viewer, click **Install**.

18. When the *PowerPoint Viewer* is installed, click **OK**.

19. Back on the *Application Virtualization – Create New Package* window, click **I am finished installing** and then click **Next**.

20. On the *Configure Software* page, click **Microsoft PowerPoint Viewer** and then click **Run Selected**. When you are prompted to load a file, click **Cancel**.

21. Back on the *Configure Software* page, click **Next**.

22. On the *Installation Report* page, click **Next**.

23. On the *Create a basic package or customize further* screen, select **Customize**. Click Next.

24. On the *Run each program briefly to optimize the package over slow or unreliable networks* screen, click **Next**. When you are prompted to continue, click **Yes**.

25. On the *Restrict operating systems for this package* screen, click **Next** to continue.

26. On the *Create Package* page, answer the following question and then click **Create**.

Question 10	*Where is the save location of the package?*

27. When the package is created, take a screen shot of the *Application Virtualization - Create Package* window by pressing **Alt+PrtScr** and then paste it into your Lab 2 worksheet file in the page provided by pressing **Ctrl+V**.

28. On the *Create Package* page, click **Close**.

29. Close the *Microsoft Application Virtualization Sequencer* window. You have completed the process for virtualizing an application.

End of exercise. Leave the computer logged in so you can complete the Lab Challenge exercise.

Lab Challenge	Deploying the App-V Program
Overview	To complete this challenge, you must demonstrate how to install the App-V Program that you created in the last exercise.
Mindset	After an App-V application is created, you must deploy it to clients. For a client to run the App-V application, you must first install the App-V client and then install the virtualized application.
Completion time	15 minutes

In the last exercise, you created an App-V program for PowerPoint Viewer. Now you will install the package on Win8B. Write the steps you would use to complete the challenge. When the PowerPoint Viewer is installed, take a screen shot of Win8B *Start* screen by pressing **Alt+PrtScr** and then paste it into your Lab 2 worksheet file in the page provided by pressing **Ctrl+V**.

End of lab.

LAB 3
SUPPORTING WINDOWS STORE AND CLOUD APPLICATIONS

THIS LAB CONTAINS THE FOLLOWING EXERCISES AND ACTIVITIES:

Exercise 3.1	Restricting Access to the Windows Store Using Group Policy
Exercise 3.2	Using AppLocker to Manage Applications
Exercise 3.3	Managing Office 365
Exercise 3.4	Managing Office 365 Users
Exercise 3.5	Creating Local Accounts
Lab Challenge	Sideloading Windows Apps

BEFORE YOU BEGIN

The lab environment consists of student workstations connected to a local area network, along with a server that functions as the domain controller for a domain called contoso.com. The computers required for this lab are listed in Table 3-1.

Table 3-1
Computers Required for Lab 3

Computer	Operating System	Computer Name
Server	Windows Server 2012 R2	RWDC01
Server	Windows Server 2012 R2	Server02
Client	Windows 8	Win8A

In addition to the computers, you will also need the software listed in Table 3-2 to complete Lab 3.

Table 3-2
Software Required for Lab 3

Software	Location
Administrative Templates (.admx) for Windows 8 and Windows Server 2012 (Windows8-Server2012ADMX-RTM.msi)	\\rwdc01\software
Lab 3 student worksheet	Lab03_worksheet.docx (provided by instructor)

Working with Lab Worksheets

Each lab in this manual requires that you answer questions, shoot screen shots, and perform other activities that you will document in a worksheet named for the lab, such as Lab03_worksheet.docx. You will find these worksheets on the book companion site. It is recommended that you use a USB flash drive to store your worksheets so you can submit them to your instructor for review. As you perform the exercises in each lab, open the appropriate worksheet file, fill in the required information, and then save the file to your flash drive.

SCENARIO

After completing this lab, you will be able to:

■ Manage Office 365 and Office 365 users

■ Restrict access to the Windows Store

■ Use AppLocker to manage applications

■ Sideload a Windows app

Estimated lab time: 95 minutes

NOTE	If you are using MOAC Labs Online, you will not be able to perform two of the exercises using an online computer. Instead, you will need use a computer running Windows 8 with access to the Internet. If your classroom has a dedicated Windows Server 2012, you can use a virtual machine running Windows 8.

Exercise 3.1	Restricting Access to the Windows Store Using Group Policy
Overview	In this exercise, you will install the Windows 8/Windows Server 2012 Administrative Templates and then use GPOs to restrict access to the Windows Store.
Mindset	While the Windows Store can provide a wide range of useful applications, these applications can cause security problems within your organization and can reduce user productivity. Therefore, you need to restrict access to the Windows Store.
Completion time	15 minutes

1. On *RWDC01*, log on using the **contoso\administrator** account and the **Pa$$w0rd** password.

2. Open **File Explorer** and navigate to the **\\rwdc01\software** folder.

3. Double-click the **Windows8.1-Server2012R2ADMX-RTM.msi** file. If you are prompted to confirm that you want to run this file, click **Run**.

4. When the *Administrative Templates for Windows Server 2012 R2 Setup Wizard* opens, click **Next**.

5. On the *License Agreement* page, click **I Agree**, and then click **Next**.

6. On the *Select Installation folder* page, answer the following question. Then click **Everyone** and click **Next**.

Question 1	What is the default installation folder?

7. On the *Confirm Installation* page, click **Next**.

8. When the installation is complete, click **Close**.

9. Using *File Explorer*, open the **C:\Program Files (x86)\Microsoft Group Policy\Windows Server2012** folder. Right-click the **PolicyDefinitions** folder and choose **Copy**.

10. Using *File Explorer*, open **\\rwdc01\sysvol\contoso.com\Policies** (see Figure 3-1).

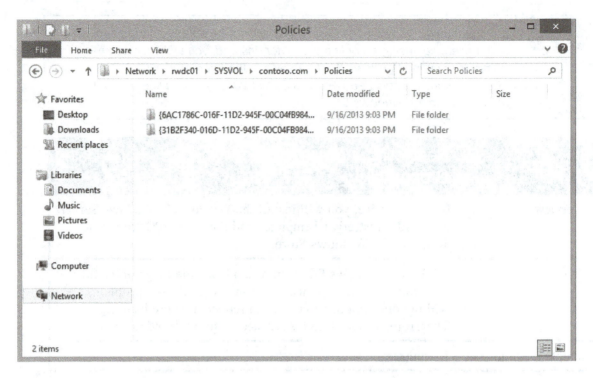

Figure 3-1
Viewing the Policies folder

11. In the *Policies* folder, right-click the empty white space and choose **Paste**.

12. Using *Server Manager*, click **Tools > Group Policy Management**.

13. On the *Group Policy Management* page, expand the **Forest: contoso.com** node, expand the **Domains** node, and then expand **contoso.com**.

14. Right-click **Default Domain Policy** and choose **Edit**.

15. On the *Group Policy Management Editor* page, navigate to **Computer Configuration > Policies > Administrative Templates > Windows Components > Store**.

16. Double-click the **Turn off the Store application** setting; the *Turn off the Store application* dialog displays. Click **Enabled**.

17. Press **Ctrl+PrtScr** to take a screen shot of the *Turn off the Store application* dialog box and the *Group Policy Management Editor* window. Press **Ctrl+V** to paste the image on the page provided in the Lab 3 worksheet file.

18. Click **OK** to close the *Turn off the Store application* dialog box. The next time the group policy settings are replicated to the client, the store will be disabled.

End of exercise. Leave the Group Policy Management Editor open for the next exercise.

Exercise 3.2	Using AppLocker to Manage Applications
Overview	In this exercise, you will use AppLocker to restrict access to an application.
Mindset	AppLocker is a powerful tool that can control which applications can be executed on a computer running Windows.
Completion time	10 minutes

1. On **RWDC01**, using the **Group Policy Management Editor** for the **Default Domain Policy**, click **Computer Configuration > Policies > Windows Settings > Security Settings > Application Control Policies > AppLocker**, as shown in Figure 3-2.

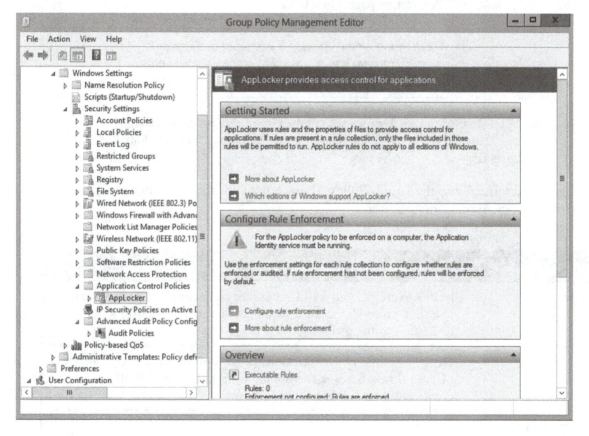

Figure 3-2
AppLocker node

2. Under the *AppLocker* node, click **Executable Rules**. Then right-click the **ExecutableRules** node and choose **Create Default Rules**. If the default rules do not show up, press the **F5** key.

Question 2	*How many rules were created?*

3. Right-click the **Executable Rules** node and choose **Create New Rule**.

4. On the *Create Executable Rules* wizard page, click **Next**.

5. On the *Permissions* page, *Allow action* is already selected and, in the *User or Group* box, *Everyone* is specified. Click **Next**.

6. On the *Conditions* page, click **Path**, and then click **Next**.

7. On the *Path* page, type **C:\Program Files\Games\sol.exe** and click **Next**.

8. On the *Exceptions* page, click **Next**.

9. On the *Name and Description* page, click **Create**.

Question 3	*Which mode would you use if you want to determine who is using a program that you want to block without actually blocking the program?*

10. Press **Ctrl+PrtScr** to take a screen shot of the *Group Policy Management Editor* window. Press **Ctrl+V** to paste the image on the page provided in the Lab 3 worksheet file.

End of exercise. Close the Group Policy Management console, and then close the Group Policy Management Editor.

Exercise 3.3	Managing Office 365
Overview	In this exercise, you will first create an account for Office 365, and then you will create a group consisting of one user and send a test email to the group.
Mindset	Office 365 is a subscription-based online office and services offered through a website aimed at organizations. It allows you to create and manage users and groups.
Completion time	30 minutes

NOTE	*If you are using MOAC Labs Online, you will not be able to perform this lab using an online computer. Instead, you will need use a computer running Windows 8 with access to the Internet. If your classroom has a dedicated Windows Server 2012 for each user, you can use a virtual machine running Windows 8.*

1. On *Win8A*, log on using the **contoso\administrator** account and the **Pa$$word** password.

2. Click the **Desktop** tile.

3. On the taskbar, click the **Internet Explorer** icon to open *Internet Explorer*.

4. Go to **http://office.microsoft.com/en-us/business/**.

5. Click **See plans & pricing**, and then click the **Enterprise** tab.

6. Under **Office 365 Enterprise E3**, click **Free trial**.

7. On the *Start your free 30-day trial* page, enter the following information:

   First Name: **<Your first name>**

   Last Name: **<Your last name>**

   Email: **<Your email address>**

   Address 1: **<Your Street Address>**

   City: **<Your city>**

   State or province: **<Your state or province>**

   Zip or postal code: **<Your zip code or postal code>**

   Phone: **<Your phone number>**

8. For the *Organization* name, type the following:

   <FirstName><LastName>Office365<Month><Year>

   Therefore, if your name is John Smith and you are performing this lab in June 2014, you would type the following:

   JohnSmithOffice365062014.onmicrosoft.com

Question 4	What is the domain name?

9. For the *User ID*, type the following:

   <FirstInitial><LastName>

   Therefore, if your name is John Smith, you would type the following:

   JSmith

10. Ensure the domain name uses the following format:

    <FirstName><LastName>Office365<Month><Year>

    Therefore, if your name is John Smith and you are performing this lab in June 2014, you would type the following:

    JohnSmithOffice365062014@onmicrosoft.com

Question 5	What is the name of the account you are creating?

11. For the *Password* text box and the *Confirm password* text box, type **Pa$$w0rd**.

12. Under *Verify your phone number*, select **Send text message**. Then type your phone number in the appropriate text box.

13. Click **create my account**.

14. If a *Don't lose access to your account* dialog box opens, type a phone number (preferably a mobile number), and then click **save and continue**.

15. In the *Verification code* text box, type the code that you receive from your phone.

16. Press **Ctrl+PrtScr** to take a screen shot of the *Office 365 admin center* screen. Press **Ctrl+V** to paste the image on the page provided in the Lab 3 worksheet file.

17. If an *It's all about you* box appears, click the small **x** to close it.

18. Click the **Office 365 settings** button (the gear button at the top-right corner of the webpage), and then click **Office 365 settings**.

19. Scroll to the bottom of the window, and then click **Save**.

20. If a *Get the most out of SharePoint* dialog box appears, click **No Thanks**.

21. At the top of the webpage, click **Outlook**.

Note	It may take a couple minutes for Microsoft to complete provision of your account. Therefore, if the Outlook link is not available, at the top of the screen, click Office 365, and then click Outlook.

Question 6	Which interface allows you to access Outlook and Calendar functionality over the Internet using a web service or webpage?

22. On the *Outlook Web App* page, select your language and time zone. Click **Save**.

23. At the top of the webpage, click **People**.

24. At the top-left corner of the window, click **New**.

25. In the *What would you like to do?* dialog box, click **create group**.

26. In the *Group name* field, type **Group1**.

27. Click **add members** and then, in the *Members* text box, type the name of the account that you specified in Step 8. Click **Search Contacts & Directory**.

28. At the top of the webpage, click **Save**.

29. Press **Ctrl+PrtScr** to take a screen shot of the *My Contacts* page. Press **Ctrl+V** to paste the image on the page provided in the Lab 3 worksheet file.

30. On the *My Contacts* page, click **Group1**. Click **members**.

31. In the right pane, click the **Send e-mail** button. If you get an Internet Explorer message indicating the email was blocked, click **Allow**.

32. In the *Subject* text box, type **Test**.

33. In the body of the email, type **Hi**, and then click **Send**.

34. At the top of the webpage, click **Outlook**. You should see the test message you just sent.

35. Press **Ctrl+PrtScr** to take a screen shot of the *Outlook* page. Press **Ctrl+V** to paste the image on the page provided in the Lab 3 worksheet file.

End of exercise. Leave Internet Explorer's Office 365 website open for the next exercise.

Exercise 3.4	Managing Office 365 Users
Overview	In this exercise, you will create a second Office 365 user and then you will create a group and add the user into the group. You will complete the exercise by managing the roles of the user and changing the password of the user.
Mindset	For larger organizations, you will need to organize the users into groups and you will need to delegate administrative tasks to other users. Some of the administrative tasks may include resetting passwords for users or creating and deleting users.
Completion time	20 minutes

> NOTE
>
> *If you are using MOAC Labs Online, you will not be able to perform this lab using an online computer. Instead, you will need use a computer running Windows 8 with access to the Internet. If your classroom has a dedicated Windows Server 2012 for each user, you can use a virtual machine running Windows 8.*

1. At the top of the webpage, click **Admin**, and then click **Office 365**.

2. In the left pane of the *Office 365 admin center* page (see Figure 3-3), click **users and groups**.

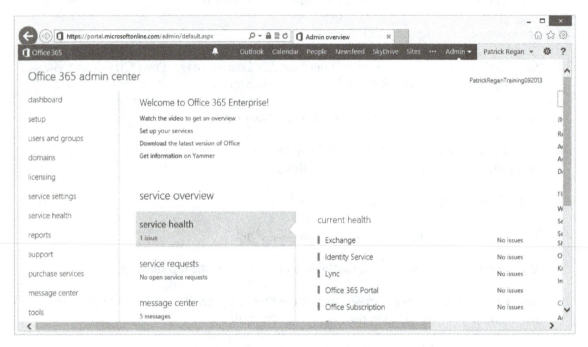

Figure 3-3
The *Office 365 admin center* page

3. At the top of the list of users, click the **Add (+)** button.

4. On the *details* page, type the following, and then click **next**.

   First name: **George**

   Last name: **Petterson**

   User name: **GPetterson**

5. On the *settings* page, click *Select a location (country)* and then click **next**.

6. On the *assign licenses* page, all licenses are selected. Answer the following questions, and then click **next**.

Question 7	How many licenses do you have?

Question 8	Which licenses are available in a Microsoft Office 365 Plan E3?

7. On the *send results in email* page, click **create**.

8. Press **Ctrl+PrtScr** to take a screen shot of the *results* page. Press **Ctrl+V** to paste the image on the page provided in the Lab 3 worksheet file.

9. Click **finish**.

10. Click **security groups**.

11. Click the **Add** (+) button.

12. On the *details* page, in the *Display name* text box, type **Sales**. Click **Save**.

13. Click to select **George Petterson**, and then click **Add**.

14. Click **ok**.

15. Press **Ctrl+PrtScr** to take a screen shot of the *security groups* page. Press **Ctrl+V** to paste the image on the page provided in the Lab 3 worksheet file.

16. Click **Save**.

17. Click **active users**.

18. Click **George Petterson**.

19. Click **settings**.

20. In the *Assign role* section, click **Yes**, and then select **Password administrator**.

Question 9	Which role would you assign to a person in the Accounting department that can be used to review and pay the bill for Office 365 for an organization?

21. In the *Alternate email address* text box, type your personal email address.

22. Click **save**.

23. On the *active users* list, click to select **George Petterson**.

24. On the right side of the screen, click **Reset passwords**.

25. On the *email* page, click **reset password**.

26. Press **Ctrl+PrtScr** to take a screen shot of the *results* page. Press **Ctrl+V** to paste the image on the page provided in the Lab 3 worksheet file.

27. Click **finish**.

28. On the left side of the webpage, click **service settings**.

29. In the menu at the top, click **passwords**.

30. In the *Days before passwords expire* field, type **100**.

31. In the *Days before a user is notified that their password will expire* field, type **20**.

32. Click **save**.

33. Close **Internet Explorer**.

End of exercise. Close any open windows before you begin the next exercise.

Exercise 3.5	Creating Local Accounts
Overview	In this exercise, you will create a user account using the Charms bar, followed by creating a user account with Computer Management.
Mindset	As an administrator, you need to know how to manage local user accounts using PC settings and Computer Management.
Completion time	10 minutes

1. On *Win8A*, point your cursor to the top-right corner of the screen to make the *Charms* bar appear.

2. Click **Settings** (the gear icon).

3. Click **Change PC Settings**.

4. Click **Accounts**, and then click **Other accounts**.

5. Click **Add an account**.

6. Click the **Sign in without a Microsoft account (not recommended)**, and then click **Local account**.

7. In the *User name* text box, type **LocalUser1**. In the *Password* text box and the *Renter password* text box, type **Pa$$w0rd**. In the *Password hint* text box, type **Standard**, and then click **Next**.

8. Click **Finish**.

9. Press the **Alt+F4** and click **Desktop** tile.

10. Right-click the **Start** button and choose **Computer Management**.

11. Under **System Tools**, expand **Local Users and Groups**.

12. Right-click the **Users** node and choose **New User**.

13. In the *User* dialog box, type the following information, and then click **Create**:

    ● *User name*: **LocalUser2**

    ● *Full name*: **Local User 2**

    ● *Password*: **Pa$$w0rd**

    ● Deselect the **User must change password at next logon**.

    ● Select **Password never expires**.

14. Click **Close**.

15. Click the **Users** container.

16. Press **Alt+PrtScr** to take a screen shot of the *Computer Management* page. Press **Ctrl+V** to paste the image on the page provided in the Lab 3 worksheet file.

17. Close **Computer Management**.

Question 10	*You have managed users using PC Settings (from the Charms bar) and by using the Computer Management. What is the third method you can use to configure local users?*

End of exercise. Leave Win8A running for the next exercise.

Lab Challenge	Sideloading a Windows App
Overview	To complete this challenge, you must demonstrate sideloading a Windows App by performing a written exercise.
	Sideloading allows an organization to upload an application to the Windows Store so that users within the organization can download the application to their Windows 8 mobile devices. To access the Windows Store, you need to have Internet access. You also need a Microsoft account in order to access the Microsoft Store, and you will need to upload an application to the store before you can download it.
Mindset	Over the last couple of months, your organization has purchased several Windows 8 tablets to be used by the sales team. The development team has created a customized application to run on the tablet. So you decide that you want to load the application on the tablet without going through the Windows Store. To do this, you use sideloading.
Completion time	10 minutes

What are the requirements to perform sideloading and what is the general process for sideloading a Windows app? Write out the steps you performed to complete the challenge. For assistance refer to Lesson 3 in the 70-688 Microsoft Official Academic Course.

End of lab.

LAB 4
SUPPORTING NETWORK CONNECTIVITY

THIS LAB CONTAINS THE FOLLOWING EXERCISES AND ACTIVITIES:

Exercise 4.1   Configuring IP Settings

Exercise 4.2   Installing and Configuring DHCP Server

Exercise 4.3   Troubleshooting DNS

Exercise 4.4   Creating a Windows Firewall Outbound Rule

Exercise 4.5   Using IP Security

Lab Challenge   Importing a Windows Firewall Rule into a GPO

BEFORE YOU BEGIN

The lab environment consists of student workstations connected to a local area network, along with a server that functions as the domain controller for a domain called contoso.com. The computers required for this lab are listed in Table 4-1.

Table 4-1
Computers Required for Lab 4

Computer	Operating System	Computer Name
Server	Windows Server 2012 R2	RWDC01
Client	Windows 8.1	Win8A
Client	Windows 8.1	Win8B

In addition to the computers, you will also need the software listed in Table 4-2 to complete Lab 4.

Table 4-2
Software Required for Lab 4

Software	Location
Lab 4 student worksheet	Lab04_worksheet.docx (provided by instructor)

Working with Lab Worksheets

Each lab in this manual requires that you answer questions, shoot screen shots, and perform other activities that you will document in a worksheet named for the lab, such as Lab04_worksheet.docx. You will find these worksheets on the book companion site. It is recommended that you use a USB flash drive to store your worksheets so you can submit them to your instructor for review. As you perform the exercises in each lab, open the appropriate worksheet file, fill in the required information, and then save the file to your flash drive.

SCENARIO

After completing this lab, you will be able to:

- ■ Configure IP settings for Windows 8

- ■ Install and configure DHCP server

- ■ Troubleshoot DNS

- ■ Create an outbound rule for Windows Firewall

- ■ Import a Windows Firewall rule into a GPO

- ■ Use IP security

Estimated lab time: 150 minutes

Exercise 4.1	Configuring IP Settings
Overview	In this exercise, you will configure the IP settings for a Windows 8.1 OS-based PC.
Mindset	As an administrator, you will need to know how to configure the IP configuration manually, including the IP address, subnet mask, default gateway, and DNS server.
Completion time	15 minutes

1. On *Win8B*, log on using the **contoso\administrator** account and the **Pa$$w0rd** password.

2. Click the **Desktop** tile.

3. Right-click the **Network Status** icon and choose **Open Network and Sharing Center**.

4. On the *Network and Sharing Center* page (as shown in Figure 4-1), click **Change adapter settings**.

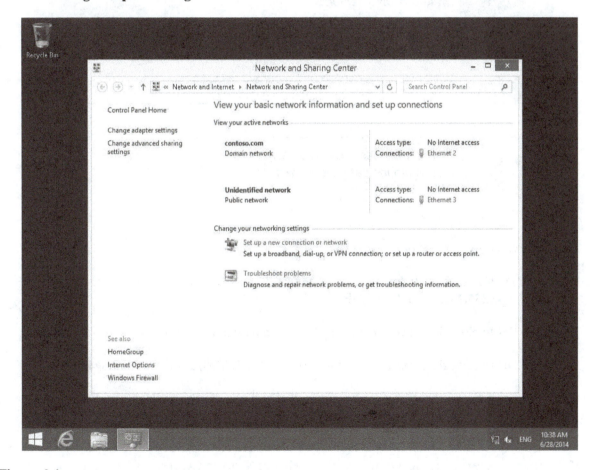

Figure 4-1
The Network and Sharing Center

5. Right-click the second **Ethernet** connection and choose **Disable**.

6. On the *Network Connections* page, double-click the first **Ethernet** connection.

7. In the *Ethernet Status* dialog box, click **Properties**.

8. In the *Ethernet Properties* dialog box, scroll down and double-click **Internet Protocol Version 4 (TCP/IPv4)**.

9. Take a screen shot of the *Internet Protocol Version 4 (TCP/IPv4) Properties* dialog box by pressing **Alt+PrtScr** and then paste it into your Lab 4 worksheet file in the page provided by pressing **Ctrl+V**.

Question 1	What is the current IP address configuration: IP address: Subnet mask: Default gateway: Preferred DNS server:

Question 2	What problem is caused by the current default gateway setting?

Question 3	What addresses could you assign to the Default gateway that would indicate a local router?

10. Click the **Advanced** button.

11. In the *IP addresses* section, click **Add**.

12. In the *TCP/IP Address* dialog box, for *IP address*, type **192.168.2.81**. For the *subnet mask*, type **255.255.255.0**. Click **Add**.

13. Click **OK** to close the *Advanced TCP/IP Settings* dialog box.

14. Click **OK** to close the *Internet Protocol Version 4 (TCP/IPv4) Properties* dialog box.

15. Click **Close** to close the *Ethernet Properties* dialog box.

16. Click **Close** to close the *Ethernet Status* dialog box.

17. Close the **Network Connections** and **Network and Sharing Center**.

18. Right-click the **Start** button and choose **Command Prompt (Admin)**.

19. In the *Command Prompt* window, execute the **ipconfig** command.

20. Take a screen shot of the *Command Prompt* window by pressing **Alt+PrtScr** and then paste it into your Lab 4 worksheet file in the page provided by pressing **Ctrl+V**.

21. Close the *Command Prompt* window.

End of exercise. Close all windows for Win8B, but leave Windows logged in for the next exercise.

Exercise 4.2	Installing and Configuring DHCP Server
Overview	In this exercise, you will install DHCP and create a DHCP scope. You will then configure a client to use the DHCP scope.
Mindset	In most organizations, Windows clients are configured using a DHCP server. Therefore, you should know how to install the DHCP services and how to create and configure DHCP scopes.
Completion time	40 minutes

First, you will install a DHCP Server by performing the following steps:

1. On *RWDC01*, log on using the **contoso\administrator** account and the **Pa$$w0rd** password.

2. Using *Server Manager*, click **Manage > Add Roles and Features**.

3. On the *Add Roles and Features Wizard* page, click **Next**.

4. On the *Select installation type* page, click **Next**.

5. On the *Select destination server* page, click **Next**.

6. On the *Select server roles* page, click to select the **DHCP Server**. When you are prompted to add features, click **Add Features**.

7. Back on the *Select server roles* page, click **Next**.

8. On the *Select features* page, click **Next**.

9. On the *DHCP Server* page, click **Next**.

10. On the *Confirm installation selections* page, click **Install**.

11. When the installation is complete, take a screen shot of the *Installation progress* page by pressing **Alt+PrtScr** and then paste it into your Lab 4 worksheet file in the page provided by pressing **Ctrl+V**.

12. Click **Close**.

Next, you will create a DHCP scope by performing the following steps:

1. On *RWDC01*, using *Server Manager*, click **Tools > DHCP**.

2. In the DHCP console, click the **rwdc01.contoso.com** node (as shown in Figure 4-2).

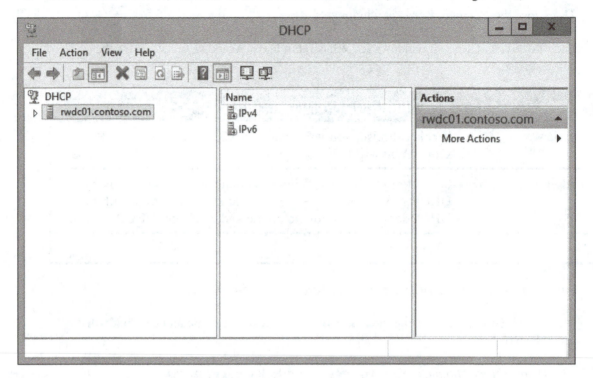

Figure 4-2
The DHCP console

3. Click **IPv4** once, then right-click **IPv4** and choose **New Scope**.

4. On the *New Scope Wizard* page, click **Next**.

5. On the *Scope Name* page in the *Name* text box, type **Normal Scope** and then click **Next**.

6. On the *IP address range* page, in the Start IP address box, type **192.168.1.40**. In the *End IP address* box, type **192.168.1.45**. For the *Subnet mask*, type **255.255.255.0**. Click **Next**.

7. On the *Add Exclusions and Delay* page, click **Next**.

8. On the *Lease Duration* page, answer the following question and then click **Next**.

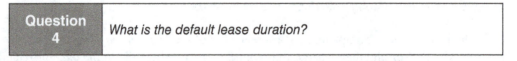

| Question 4 | What is the default lease duration? |

9. On the *Configure DHCP Options* page, click **Next**.

10. On the *Router (Default Gateway)* page, in the *IP address* box, type **192.168.1.20** and then click **Add**. Click **Next**.

11. On the *Domain Name and DNS Servers* page, remove any IP addresses. In the *IP address* box, ensure that **192.168.1.50** is specified for the DNS server IP address Click **Next**.

12. On the *WINS Servers* page, click **Next**.

13. On the *Activate Scope* page, click **Next**.

14. When the wizard is complete, click **Finish**.

Question 5	*Although you have activated the scope, the server is still not ready to assign DHCP addresses. Therefore, what major step still needs to be performed so that the DHCP server can assign IP addresses? (Hint: the DHCP console tells you what must be done)*

15. Right-click **rwdc01.contoso.com** and choose **Authorize**.

16. Press the **F5** key to refresh the *DHCP* console.

17. Take a screen shot of the *DHCP* console showing the new created scope by pressing **Alt+PrtScr** and then paste it into your Lab 4 worksheet file in the page provided by pressing **Ctrl+V**.

Next, you will configure a Client to use DHCP by performing the following steps:

1. On *Win8B*, right-click the **Network Status** icon and choose **Open Network and Sharing Center**.

2. On the *Network and Sharing Center* page, click **Change adapter settings**.

3. In the *Network Connections* dialog box, double-click the first **Ethernet** connection.

4. In the *Ethernet Status* dialog box, click **Properties**.

5. In the *Ethernet Properties* dialog box, scroll down and double-click **Internet Protocol Version 4 (TCP/IPv4)**.

6. Click to select **Obtain an IP address automatically**.

7. Click to select **Obtain DNS server address automatically**.

8. Click **OK** to close the *Internet Protocol Version 4 (TCP/IP) Properties* dialog box.

9. Click **OK** to close the *Ethernet Properties* dialog box and click **Close** to close the Ethernet Status dialog box.

10. Right-click the **Start** button and choose **Command Prompt (Admin)**.

11. In the *Command Prompt* window, execute the **ipconfig** command.

12. Take a screen shot of the *Command Prompt* window by pressing **Alt+PrtScr** and then paste it into your Lab 4 worksheet file in the page provided by pressing **Ctrl+V**.

Question 6	Which IPv4Address was assigned?

13. At the command prompt, execute the **ipconfig /all** command.

Question 7	What is the IP Address of the DHCP server?

Lastly, you will use Automatic IP address assignment by performing the following steps:

1. On *RWDC01*, using the *DHCP* console, click, and then right-click the **192.168.1.0** scope and choose **Deactivate**. When you are prompted to disable the scope, click **Yes**.

2. On *Win8B*, at the command prompt, execute the **ipconfig /release** command.

3. At the command prompt, execute the **ipconfig /renew** command. This command may take a couple of minutes to complete.

4. Execute the **ipconfig** command.

5. Take a screen shot of the *Command Prompt* window by pressing **Alt+PrtScr** and then paste it into your Lab 4 worksheet file in the page provided by pressing **Ctrl+V**.

Question 8	Which address did the computer receive?

Question 9	Typically, when you see that a computer has an address that begins with 169.254, what is the problem?

6. On *RWDC01*, using the *DHCP* console, right-click the **192.168.1.0** scope and choose **Activate**.

7. On *Win8B*, execute the **ipconfig /renew** command.

End of exercise. On Win8B, leave the *Command Prompt* window open so you can perform the next exercise. On RWDC01, close all windows.

Exercise 4.3	Troubleshooting DNS
Overview	In Exercise 5.3, you will use nslookup and the DNS console to test DNS.
Mindset	When users cannot resolve IP addresses by host name, users cannot access more resources and services. When these problems occur, you should check if the user is pointing to the correct DNS server . Also, they need to know how to use the available troubleshooting tools, such as nslookup.
Completion time	15 minutes

1. On *Win8B*, on the *Network Connections* page, double-click the first **Ethernet** connection.

2. In the *Ethernet Status* dialog box, click **Properties**.

3. In the *Ethernet Properties* dialog box, scroll down and double-click **Internet Protocol Version 4 (TCP/IPv4)**.

4. Configure the following:

   IP address: **192.168.1.81**

   Subnet mask: **255.255.255.0**

   Preferred DNS server: **192.168.1.50**

5. Click **OK** to close the *Internet Protocol (TCP/IPv4) Properties* dialog box. Then click **OK** to close *Ethernet Properties*. Click **Close** to close *Ethernet Status*.

6. On *Win8B*, at the command prompt, execute the **Nslookup win8a.contoso.com** command.

Question 10	Which IPv4 address is assigned to win8a.contoso.com?

7. To start nslookup in interactive mode, execute the **Nslookup** command.

Question 11	Which address is the DNS server?

8. To look up the address of *win8a.contoso.com*, execute the **win8a** command at the nslookup prompt.

9. To display the SOA record for the *contoso.com* domain, execute the following commands at the nslookup prompt:

```
set type=soa

contoso.com
```

10. Take a screen shot of the *Command Prompt - nslookup* window by pressing **Alt+PrtScr** and then paste it into your Lab 4 worksheet file in the page provided by pressing **Ctrl+V**.

11. Close the *Command Prompt* window.

12. On *RWDC01*, using *Server Manager*, click **Tools > DNS**.

13. In the *DNS Manager* console, click, and then right-click **RWDC01** and choose **Properties**. The *Properties* dialog box appears.

14. Click the **Monitoring** tab (see Figure 4-3).

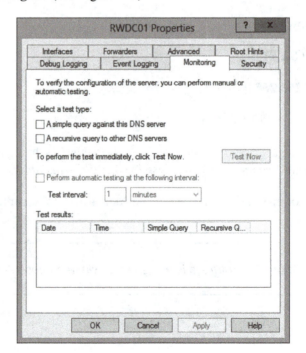

Figure 4-3
The Monitoring tab

15. Select the following settings:

    A simple query against this DNS server

    A recursive query to other DNS servers

16. Click **Test Now**.

17. Take a screen shot of the *RWDC01 Properties* dialog box by pressing **Alt+PrtScr** and then paste it into your Lab 4 worksheet file in the page provided by pressing **Ctrl+V**.

Question 12	Did either the simple query or the recursive query fail? If a failure did occur, why did it fail?

18. Click **OK** to close *RWDC01 Properties* dialog box, then close **DNS Manager**.

End of exercise. Leave Win8B logged on for the next exercise. Log off RWDC01.

Exercise 4.4	Creating a Windows Firewall Outbound Rule
Overview	In this exercise, you will create a Windows Firewall outbound rule.
Mindset	By default, Windows Firewall allows only certain packets from the computer. Therefore, you must know how to adjust the firewall to allow additional outgoing packets as needed.
Completion time	10 minutes

1. On *Win8B*, right-click the **Start** menu and choose **Control Panel**.

2. In *Control Panel*, click **System and Security**.

3. Under *System and Security*, click **Windows Firewall**.

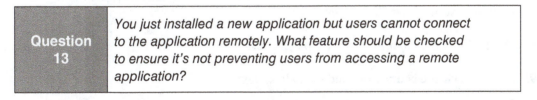

Question 13	You just installed a new application but users cannot connect to the application remotely. What feature should be checked to ensure it's not preventing users from accessing a remote application?

4. On the *Windows Firewall* page (see Figure 4-4), in the left pane, click **Advanced settings**.

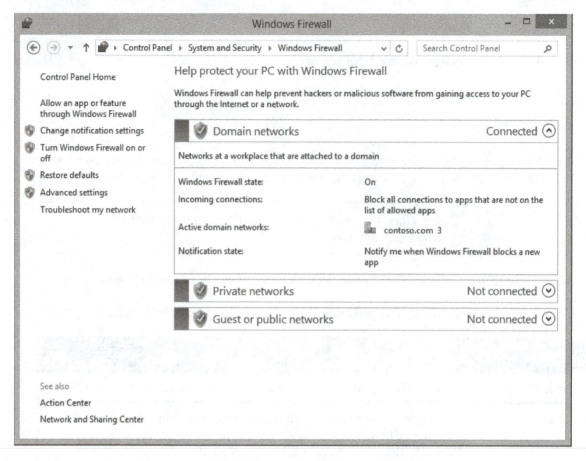

Figure 4-4
Windows Firewall

5. Click **Outbound Rules** once, then right-click **Outbound Rules** and choose **New Rule**.

6. Select **Program** and then click **Next**.

7. Click **Browse** and then navigate to the location of your installation of Internet Explorer. This can usually be found at *\%ProgramFiles%\Internet Explorer\iexplore.exe*. Click **iexplore.exe** and then click **Open**.

8. On the *New Outbound Rule Wizard* page, click **Next**.

9. Select **Block the connection** and then click **Next**.

10. Select **Domain, Private, and Public** and then click **Next**.

11. For the name of the profile, type **IE Restriction**; for the description, type **Restricts IE from connecting to the Internet**.

12. Click **Finish**.

13. Take a screen shot of the *Windows Firewall with Advanced Security* window by pressing **Alt+PrtScr** and then paste it into your Lab 4 worksheet file in the page provided by pressing **Ctrl+V**.

14. Right-click the **IE Restriction** rule and choose **Disable Rule**.

End of exercise. Leave Win8B logged in for the next exercise.

Exercise 4.5	Using IP Security
Overview	In this exercise, you will configure IP Security for a computer running Windows 8.1, so that ICMP traffic is encrypted.
Mindset	IP security (IPsec) is a suite of protocols that provides a mechanism for data integrity, authentication, and privacy for the Internet Protocol by providing message authentication and/or encryption. If you require secure communications even within a local network, you can configure IP Security (IPsec) to encrypt any specified traffic.
Completion time	40 minutes

1. On *Win8B*, using *Windows Firewall with Advanced Security*, click, and then right-click **Inbound Rules** and then click **New Rule**.

2. In the *New Inbound Rule Wizard* dialog box, on the *Rule Type* page, click **Custom**, and then click **Next**.

3. On the *Program* page, click **Next**.

4. On the *Protocols and Ports* page, in the *Protocol type* list, select **ICMPv4** and then click **Next**.

5. On the *Scope* page, click **Next**.

6. On the *Action* page, click **Allow the connection if it is secure**, and then click **Next**.

7. On the *Users* page, click **Next**.

8. On the *Computers* page, click **Next**.

9. On the *Profile* page, click **Next**.

10. On the *Name* page, in the *Name* box, type **ICMPv4 Allowed** and then click **Finish**.

11. Log on to *Win8A* using the **contoso\administrator** account and the **Pa$$w0rd** password.

12. Using *Windows Firewall with Advanced Security*, click, and then right-click **Connection Security Rules**, and then click **New Rule**.

13. Click **Desktop**, and then right-click the **Start** menu and choose **Control Panel**.

14. In *Control Panel*, click **System and Security**. Under *System and Security*, click **Windows Firewall**.

15. On the *Windows Firewall* page, in the left pane, click **Advanced settings**.

16. Click, and then right-click **Connection Security Rules**, and then click **New Rule**.

17. When the New *Connection Security Rule Wizard* opens, on the *Rule Type* page, click **Server-to-Server** and then click **Next**.

18. On the *Endpoints* page, click **Next**.

19. On the *Requirements* page, **click Require authentication for inbound and outbound connections** and then click **Next**.

Question 14	When using IPsec, how can you ensure that each computer uses its own private key pair?

20. On the *Authentication Method* page, click **Advanced**, and then click **Customize**.

21. In the *Customize Advanced Authentication Methods* dialog box, under *First authentication*, click **Add**.

22. In the *Add First Authentication Method* dialog box, click **Preshared Key**, type **secret**, and then click **OK**.

23. In the *Customize Advanced Authentication Methods* dialog box, click **OK**.

24. On the *Authentication Method* page, click **Next**.

25. On the *Profile* page, click **Next**.

26. On the *Name* page, in the *Name* box, type **Client to Client**, and then click **Finish**.

27. On *Win8B*, click, and then right-click **Connection Security Rules**, and then click **New Rule**.

28. In the *New Connection Security Rule Wizard*, on the *Rule Type* page, click **Server-to-Server**, and then click **Next**.

29. On the *Endpoints* page, click **Next**.

30. On the *Requirements* page, click **Require authentication for inbound and outbound connections**, and then click **Next**.

31. On the *Authentication Method* page, click **Advanced**, and then click **Customize**.

32. In the *Customize Advanced Authentication Methods* dialog box, under *First authentication*, click **Add**.

33. In the *Add First Authentication Method* dialog box, click **Preshared Key**, type **secret**, and then click **OK**.

34. In the *Customize Advanced Authentication Methods* dialog box, click **OK**.

35. On the *Authentication Method* page, click **Next**.

36. On the *Profile* page, click **Next**.

37. On the *Name* page, in the *Name* box, type **Client to Client**, and then click **Finish**.

38. Take a screen shot of the *Windows Firewall with Advanced Security* window showing the *Connection Security Rules* by pressing **Alt+PrtScr** and then paste it into your Lab 4 worksheet file in the page provided by pressing **Ctrl+V**.

39. On *Win8A*, right-click **Start** and choose **Command Prompt (Admin)**.

40. At the command prompt, type ping **192.168.1.81**, and then press **Enter**.

41. Switch to *Windows Firewall with Advanced Security*. Expand **Monitoring**, expand **Security Associations**, and then click **Main Mode**.

42. In the right-pane, double-click the listed item. View the information in **Main Mode**, and then click **OK**.

43. Expand **Quick Mode**.

44. Take a screen shot of the *Windows Firewall with Advanced Security* window showing the Quick Mode node by pressing **Alt+PrtScr** and then paste it into your Lab 4 worksheet file in the page provided by pressing **Ctrl+V**.

45. In the right-pane, double-click the listed item. View the information in **Quick Mode**, and then click **OK**.

46. On *Win8A*, click **Connection Security Rules** node under *Windows Firewall with Advanced Security*. Do not click the *Connection Security Rules under Monitoring*.

47. Right-click the **Client to Client** security rule and choose **Delete**. When prompted to delete this rule, click **Yes**.

48. On *Win8B*, under *Windows Firewall with Advanced Security*, click the **Connection Security Rules** node. Under *Monitoring*, do not click the *Connection Security Rules*.

49. Right-click the **Client to Client** security rule and choose **Delete**. When prompted to delete this rule, click **Yes**.

50. Click the **Inbound Rules** node.

51. Right-click the **ICMPv4 Allowed rule** and choose **Delete**. When prompted to delete this rule, click **Yes**.

End of exercise. Leave Win8B logged in for the next exercise.

Lab Challenge	Importing a Windows Firewall Rule into a GPO
Overview	To complete this challenge, you will import the Windows Firewall rule you created in Exercise 5.4 into a GPO. Then you will apply the GPO to the Sales OU. If the Sales OU does not exist, you must create the Sales OU and move the computer Win8A into the Sales OU.
Mindset	You are the administrator for the Contoso Corporation. Since you created a Windows Firewall rule in the last exercise, you need to save that into a GPO so that it can be automatically applied to the users.
Completion time	20 minutes

Write out the steps you performed to complete the challenge. Take a screen shot of the final *Group Policy Management* console, and take a screen shot to confirm Win8A Windows Firewall with Advanced Security Outbound Rules includes the IE Restriction rule.

End of lab.

LAB 5
SUPPORTING REMOTE ACCESS

THIS LAB CONTAINS THE FOLLOWING EXERCISES AND ACTIVITIES

Exercise 5.1   Installing and Configuring RRAS

Exercise 5.2   Configuring a VPN Server

Exercise 5.3   Configuring a VPN Client

Exercise 5.4   Resetting Servers

Exercise 5.5   Using Connection Manager Administration Kit (CMAK)

Exercise 5.6   Installing Remote Server Administration Tools for Windows 8.1

Lab Challenge   Deploying DirectAccess

BEFORE YOU BEGIN

The lab environment consists of student workstations connected to a local area network, along with a server that functions as the domain controller for a domain called contoso.com. The computers required for this lab are listed in Table 5-1.

Table 5-1
Computers Required for Lab 5

Computer	Operating System	Computer Name
Server	Windows Server 2012 R2	RWDC01
Server	Windows Server 2012 R2	Server02
Client	Windows Server 8.1	Win8B

In addition to the computers, you will also need the software listed in Table 5-2 to complete Lab 5.

Table 5-2
Software Required for Lab 5

Software	Location
Remote Server Administrative Tools for Windows 8.1 (Windows8.1-KB2693643-x64.msu)	\\rwdc01\software
Lab 5 student worksheet	Lab05_worksheet.docx (provided by instructor)

Working with Lab Worksheets

Each lab in this manual requires that you answer questions, shoot screen shots, and perform other activities that you will document in a worksheet named for the lab, such as Lab05_worksheet.docx. You will find these worksheets on the book companion site. It is recommended that you use a USB flash drive to store your worksheets so you can submit them to your instructor for review. As you perform the exercises in each lab, open the appropriate worksheet file, fill in the required information, and then save the file to your flash drive.

SCENARIO

After completing this lab, you will be able to:

■ Install and configure RRAS

■ Configure a VPN server and a VPN client

■ Connect to a VPN server using a Windows 8 client

■ Disable Routing and Remote Access.

■ Create and deploy a CMAK package

■ Deploy DirectAccess

Estimated lab time: 135 minutes

Exercise 5.1	Installing and Configuring RRAS
Overview	Routing and Remote Access Server (RRAS) is used to configure standard VPN connection. In this exercise, you will install RRAS on Server02.
Mindset	RRAS allows users to connect to a server remotely through a dial-up or a VPN. It can also provide Network Address Translation (NAT) and routing.
Completion time	15 minutes

1. On *Server02*, log on using the **contoso\administrator** account and the **Pa$$w0rd** password. The *Server Manager* console opens.

2. On *Server Manager*, click **Manage > Add Roles and Features**. The *Add Roles and Features Wizard* opens.

3. On the *Before you begin page*, click **Next**.

4. Select **Role-based or feature-based installation** and then click **Next**.

5. On the *Select destination server* page, click **Next**.

6. On the *Select server roles* page, click to select the **Remote Access** checkbox. Click **Next**.

7. On the *Select features* page, click **Next**.

8. On the *Remote Access* page, click **Next**.

9. On the *Select role services* page select **DirectAccess and VPN (RAS)** and **Routing**. When you are prompted to add features, click **Add Features**. Click **Next**.

10. On the *Confirm installation selections* page, click **Install**.

11. When the installation is complete, take a screen shot of the *Results* page by pressing **Alt+PrtScr** and then paste it into your Lab 5 worksheet file in the page provided by pressing **Ctrl+V**.

12. Click **Close**.

End of exercise. You can leave any windows open for the next exercise.

Exercise 5.2	Configuring a VPN Server
Overview	In this exercise, you will configure Server02 to be a VPN server so users can connect to it over an insecure network.
Mindset	After you install Routing and Remote Access, you must then configure Routing and Remote settings to support VPN connections.
Completion time	30 minutes

1. On *Server02*, on the taskbar, right-click the **Network Status** icon and choose **Open Network and Sharing Center**.

2. Click **Change adapter settings**.

3. Right-click the first Ethernet connection and choose **Rename**. Change the name to **Internal** and then press **Enter**.

4. Right-click the second Ethernet connection and choose **Rename**. Change the name to **External** and then press **Enter**.

5. Right-click **External** and choose **Properties**.

6. In the *External Properties* dialog box, double-click **Internet Protocol Version 4 (TCP/IPv4)**.

7. For the following settings, specify the following and then click **OK**:

   IP address: **192.168.2.1**

   Subnet mask: **255.255.255.0**

8. Click **OK** to close the *External Properties* dialog box.

9. Close **Network Connections** and then close **Network and Sharing Center**.

10. On **Server02**, using *Server Manager*, click **Tools > Routing and Remote Access**. The *Routing and Remote Access* console opens (see Figure 5-1).

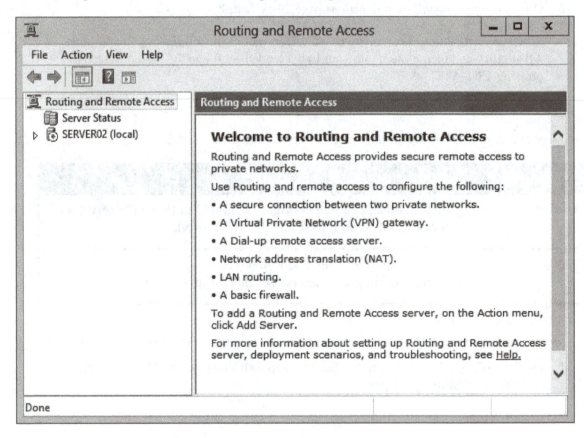

Figure 5-1
The Routing and Remote Access console

11. Right-click **Server02** and choose **Configure and Enable Routing and Remote Access**. The *Routing and Remote Access Server Setup Wizard* opens.

12. On the *Welcome* page, click **Next**.

13. On the *Configuration* page, select **Virtual private network (VPN) access and NAT** and click **Next**.

14. On the *VPN Connection* page, select **External** and then click **Next**.

15. On the *IP Address Assignment* page, click **From a specified range of addresses** and then click **Next**.

16. On the *Address Range Assignment* page, click **New**.

17. In the *New IPv4 Address Range* dialog box, specify the *Start IP address* as **192.168.1.30** and the *End IP address* as **192.168.1.35**. Click **OK**.

18. Back on the *Address Range Assignment* page, click **Next**.

19. On the *Managing Multiple Remote Access Servers* page, click **Next**.

20. On the *Completing the Routing and Remote Access Server Setup Wizard* page, click **Finish**.

21. When you are prompted to open a port of Routing and Remote Access in the Windows Firewall, click **OK**.

22. When you are prompted to support the relaying of DHCP messages from remote access clients message, click **OK**.

23. Take a screen shot of the *Routing and Remote Access* window by pressing **Alt+PrtScr** and then paste it into your Lab 5 worksheet file in the page provided by pressing **Ctrl+V**.

24. After RRAS starts, click the **Start** button, and then click the **Administrative Tools** tile.

25. On the *Administrative Tools* page, scroll down to and double-click **Windows Firewall with Advanced Security**.

26. On the *Windows Firewall with Advanced Security* page, under **Actions**, click **Properties**.

27. In the *Windows Firewall with Advanced Security on Local Computer* dialog box, with the *Domain Profile* tab selected, change the *Firewall state* to **Off**.

28. On the *Private profile* tab and the *Public Profile* tab, change the *Firewall state* to **Off**.

29. Click **OK** to close the *Windows Firewall with Advanced Security on Local Computer* dialog box.

30. Close *Windows Firewall with Advanced Security* and *Administrative Tools*.

31. Back in the *Routing and Remote Access* window, expand **SERVER02**, and then right-click **Ports** and choose **Properties**. The *Ports Properties* dialog box appears.

Question 1	By default, how many IKEv2 connections are available?

32. Click **OK** to close the *Ports Properties* dialog box.

33. Log on to *RWDC01* using the **contoso\administrator** account and the **Pa$$w0rd** password.

34. On *Server Manager*, click **Tools > Active Directory Users and Computers**.

35. Expand **contoso.com**, if needed, and then click **Users**.

36. Double-click the **Administrator** account. The *Administrator Properties* dialog box opens.

37. Click the **Dial-in** tab.

Question 2	What is the default setting for Network Access Permission?

38. In the *Network Access Permission* section, click to select **Allow access**.

39. Take a screen shot of the *Administrator Properties* window by pressing **Alt+PrtScr** and then paste it into your Lab 5 worksheet file in the page provided by pressing **Ctrl+V**.

40. Click **OK** to close the *Administrator Properties* dialog box.

End of exercise. You can leave any windows open for the next exercise.

Exercise 5.3	Configuring a VPN Client
Overview	Now that you have configured the VPN server, you need to configure a client to connect to the VPN server. In this exercise, you will use Win8B to act as a VPN client.
Mindset	After the server is created, you have to go to each client and configure the VPN connection that can be used to connect to the VPN server.
Completion time	25 minutes

1. On *Win8B*, log on using the **contoso\administrator** account and the **Pa$$w0rd** password.

2. Click the **Desktop** tile.

3. On *Win8B*, on the taskbar, right-click the **Network Status** icon and choose **Open Network and Sharing Center**.

4. Click **Change adapter settings**.

5. Right-click first **Ethernet** connection and choose **Disable**.

6. Ensure that the second **Ethernet** adapter is enabled. If it is not, right-click the second **Ethernet** connection, and choose **Enable**.

7. Right-click second **Ethernet** connection and choose **Properties**.

8. In the *Ethernet 3 Properties* dialog box, double-click **Internet Protocol Version 4 (TCP/IPv4)**.

9. Specify the following options and then click **OK**:

    IP address: **192.168.2.10**

    Subnet mask: **255.255.255.0**

    Do not change the DNS settings

10. Click **OK** to close the *Ethernet 3 Properties* dialog box.

11. Close **Network Connections**.

12. On Win8B, in the *Network and Sharing Center*, choose **Set up a new connection or network**.

13. On the *Set Up a Connection or Network* page, choose **Connect to a workplace**, and then click **Next**.

14. On the *Connect to a Workplace* page, click **Use my Internet connection (VPN)**.

15. If you are prompted to set up an Internet connection, click **I'll set up an Internet connection later**.

16. When you are prompted to type the Internet address to connect to, in the *Internet address* text box, type **192.168.2.1** and then click **Create**.

17. In the *Networks* pane (as shown in Figure 5-2), click **VPN Connection** and then click **Connect**.

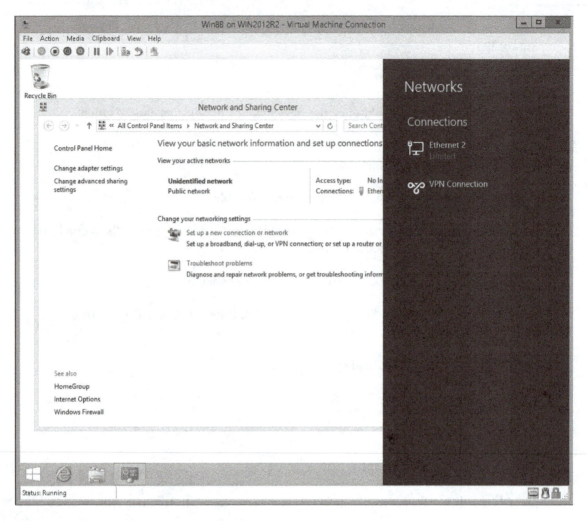

Figure 5-2
Clicking a VPN connection

18. Log on using the **contoso\Administrator** and **Pa$$w0rd** password. Click **OK**. A minute or two might pass before you are connected.

19. Take a screen shot of the *Networks* pane showing a successful connection by pressing **Alt+PrtScr** and then paste it into your Lab 5 worksheet file in the page provided by pressing **Ctrl+V**.

20. Click **VPN Connection** and then click **Disconnect**.

Question 3	*A user says that he cannot connect to the VPN server from home. Since the client will connect over the Internet, what is the first thing that you should check that the client should be able to do?*

21. Going back to *RWDC01*, using *Active Directory Users and Computers*, double-click the **Administrator** account.

22. In the *Administrator Properties* dialog box, click the **Dial-in** tab.

23. In the *Network Access Permission* section, click **Control access through NPS Network Policy**.

24. Click **OK** to close the *Administrator Properties* dialog box.

25. On *Win8B*, click the **Network and Sharing Center** icon on the taskbar, click **VPN Connection,** click **Disconnect**, and then click **Connect**.

Question 4	What error message did you get?

26. Close the **Network and Sharing Center**.

27. Going back to *RWDC01*, using *Active Directory Users and Computers*, double-click the **Administrator** account.

28. In the *Administrator Properties* dialog box, click the **Dial-in** tab.

29. In the *Network Access Permission* section, click **Allow access**.

30. Click **OK** to close the *Administrator Properties* dialog box.

31. On *Server02*, open **Administrative Tools** and then double-click **Windows Firewall with Advanced Security**.

32. In the *Windows Firewall with Advanced Security* console, under Actions, click **Properties**.

33. On the *Domain Profile* tab, change the *Firewall state* to **On**.

34. Using the *Private Profile* and *Public Profile* tabs, turn the Firewall state to **On**.

35. Click **OK** to close the *Windows Firewall with Advanced Security* console.

36. On *Win8B*, click the **Network and Sharing Center** icon on the taskbar.

37. Click **VPN Connection** and then click **Connect**.

Question 5	What error message did you get?

38. Close **Network and Sharing Center**.

39. On *Server01*, using *Windows Firewall with Advanced Security*, under *Actions*, click **Properties**.

40. On the **Domain Profile** tab, change the *Firewall state* to **Off**.

41. Using the *Private Profile* and *Public Profile* tabs, turn the *Firewall state* to **Off**.

42. Click **OK** to close the *Windows Firewall with Advanced Security* console.

End of exercise. You can leave any windows open for the next exercise.

Exercise 5.4	Resetting Servers
Overview	Before you can continue to the next exercise, you need to disable Routing and Remote Access so that it will not interfere with future exercises.
Mindset	If you need to stop the Routing and Remote Access server's operation, you simply have to disable Routing and Remote Access.
Completion time	5 minutes

1. On *Server02*, with *Routing and Remote Access* already open, right-click **Server02** and choose **Disable Routing and Remote Access** (see Figure 5-3).

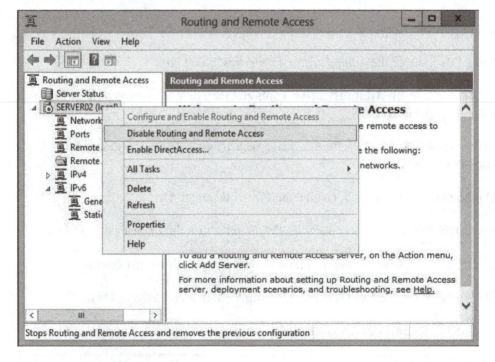

Figure 5-3
Disabling Routing and Remote Access

2. When you are prompted to continue, click **Yes**.

3. After *RRAS* stops, take a screen shot of the *Routing and Remote Access* window by pressing **Alt+PrtScr** and then paste it into your Lab 5 worksheet file in the page provided by pressing **Ctrl+V**.

4. Close **Routing and Remote Access**.

5. On *Win8B*, on the taskbar, right-click the **Network Status** icon and choose **Networking and Sharing Center**.

6. Click **Change adapter settings**.

7. Right-click **Ethernet 2** and choose **Enable**.

8. Close **Network Connections** and close **Network and Sharing Center**.

End of exercise. Close all windows on Server02 and Win8B. However, leave Server02 logged in for the next exercise.

Exercise 5.5	Using Connection Manager Administration Kit (CMAK)
Overview	In this exercise, to help deploy VPN connections to clients, you will use Connection Manager Administration Kit (CMAK) to create an installation executable that can be deployed to clients that will contain a predefined VPN connection.
Mindset	The Connection Manager simplifies configuring a client computer's VPN connection by using profiles with connection settings that allow local computers to connect to a remote network. When done, you would then distribute the created executable file to the client computers.
Completion time	30 minutes

1. On *Server02*, using *Server Manager*, click **Tools > Connection Manager Administration Kit**.

2. On the *CMAK Wizard* page, click **Next**.

3. On the *Select the Target Operating System* page, click **Next**.

4. On the *Create or Modify a Connection Manager* profile page, click **Next**.

5. In both the *Service name* field and the *File name* field, type **MyVPN** and then click **Next**.

6. On the *Specify a Realm Name* page, click **Next**.

7. On the *Merge Information from Other Profiles* page, click **Next**.

8. On the *Add Support for VPN Connections* page, click to select the **Phone book from this profile**. With the Always use the same VPN server option already selected, in the *Always use the same VPN server* text box, type **192.168.2.1** and then click **Next**.

9. On the *Create or Modify a VPN Entry* page, *MyVPN Tunnel <Default>* is already highlighted. Click **Edit**.

10. In the *Edit VPN Entry* dialog box, click the **Security** tab.

Question 6	By default, which authentication method is supported?

11. Click the **Advanced** button. If you are required to use a preshared key, you would select the **Use a preshared key** option. For now, click **OK**.

12. Click the **Advanced** tab.

13. In the *DNS suffix for this connection setting* text box, type **contoso.com**. Click **OK**.

14. Back on the *Create or Modify a VPN Entry* page, click **Next**.

15. On the *Add a Custom Phone Book* page, deselect **Automatically download phone book updates** and then click **Next**.

16. On the *Configure Dial-up Networking Entries* page, click **Next**.

17. On the *Specify Routing Table Updates* page, click **Next**.

18. On the *Configure Proxy Settings for Internet Explorer* page, click **Next**.

19. On the *Add Custom Actions* page, click **Next**.

20. On the *Display a Custom Logon Bitmap* page, click **Next**.

21. On the *Display a Custom Phone Book Bitmap* page, click **Next**.

22. On the *Display Custom Icons* page, click **Next**.

23. On the *Include a Custom Help File* page, click **Next**.

24. On the *Display Custom Support Information* page, click **Next**.

25. On the *Display a Custom License Agreement* page, click **Next**.

26. On the *Install Additional Files with the Connection Manager profile* page, click **Next**.

27. On the *Build the Connection Manager Profile and Its Installation Program* page, click **Next**.

Question 7	Where is the executable stored?

28. Take a screen shot of the *Connection Manager Administration Kit Wizard* by pressing **Alt+PrtScr** and then paste it into your Lab 5 worksheet file in the page provided by pressing **Ctrl+V**.

29. Click **Finish**.

30. On the taskbar, click the **File Explorer** icon.

31. In *File Explorer*, navigate to the **C:\Program Files\CMAK\Profiles\Windows Vista and above** folder.

32. Double-click the **MyVPN** folder.

33. Right-click the **MyVPN** application and choose **Copy**.

34. Using *File Explorer*, open the **\\rwdc01\software** folder.

35. Right-click the white space inside the software folder and choose **Paste**.

36. On *Win8B*, on the taskbar, click the **Network Status** icon and then select **Open Network and Sharing Center**.

37. In the *Network and Sharing Center*, click **Change adapter settings**.

38. Right-click **Ethernet 3** and choose **Disable**.

39. Right-click **Ethernet 2** and choose **Enable**.

40. Using *File Explorer*, open the **\\rwdc01\software\MyVPN** folder.

41. Double-click the **MyVPN** application. When you are prompted to install MyVPN, click **Yes**.

42. In the *MyVPN* dialog box, select **All users** and then click **OK**.

43. Take a screen shot of the *Network Connections* folder by pressing **Alt+PrtScr** and then paste it into your Lab 5 worksheet file in the page provided by pressing **Ctrl+V**.

End of exercise. You can leave any windows open for the next exercise.

Exercise 5.6	Installing Remote Server Administration Tools for Windows 8.1
Overview	In this exercise, you will install the Remote Server Administration Tools for Windows 8.1 on a client computer so that you can perform many of the Active Directory and server administration tasks from a client computer.
Mindset	By installing Remote Server Administration Tools for Windows 8.1, you can perform many of the Active Directory and server administration tasks from a client computer.
Completion time	15 minutes

1. On *Win8B*, open *File Explorer* by clicking the **File Explorer** icon on the taskbar. Then, using *File Explorer,* open the **\\rwdc01\software** folder.

2. Double-click the **Windows8.1-KB2693643-x64.msu** file.

3. When you are prompted to open the file, click **Open**.

4. When you are prompted to install the update, click **Yes**.

5. When *Read these license terms* appears, click **I Accept**.

6. When the installation is complete, click **Close**.

7. Click the **Start** screen thumbnail to open the *Start* menu. Then click the down arrow to show all programs, scroll over to the **Windows System** section, and then click **Administrative Tools**. The *Administrative Tools* folder opens.

8. Take a screen shot of the *Administrative Tools* folder by pressing **Alt+PrtScr** and then paste it into your Lab 5 worksheet file in the page provided by pressing **Ctrl+V**.

Question 8	*If you compare the tools that are on RWDC01, why are there additional tools on Win8B not found on RWDC01?*

9. In the *Administrative Tools* window, double-click **Active Directory Users and Computers**.

10. Expand **contoso.com**, click the **Users** OU, and then view the users that you have been using.

11. Close **Active Directory Users and Computers**.

End of exercise. Close all windows except the *Administrative Tools* window and leave Win8B logged in for the next exercise.

Lab Challenge	Deploying DirectAccess
Overview	To complete this challenge, you will demonstrate your understanding of how to use DirectAccess by running the DirectAccess Getting Started Wizard on Server02.
	If you are working on the MOAC Labs Online, you'll be able to step through the lab until you need access to the Internet with a public IP Address. Because the MOAC Labs Online do not provide Internet access, you will not be able to complete the ending steps. You can perform the lab on a computer with Remote Access Management installed.
	If you need assistance with deploying DirectAccess, refer to Lesson 5 of the 70-688 Microsoft Official Academic Course.
Mindset	DirectAccess is a more advanced form of a VPN that offers automatic VPN connections to an organization over the Internet. To keep the VPN connections secure, DirectAccess uses IPSec. Different from configure a VPN client using Routing and Remote Access, DirectAccess requires IPv6.
Completion time	15 minutes

On Server02, you have already installed the Remote Access Management. Therefore, to configure DirectAccess quickly, use the DirectAccess Getting Started Wizard. Write out the steps you performed to complete the challenge.

End of lab.

LAB 6
SUPPORTING AUTHENTICATION AND AUTHORIZATION

THIS LAB CONTAINS THE FOLLOWING EXERCISES AND ACTIVITIES:

Exercise 6.1	Requesting a Digital Certificate
Exercise 6.2	Creating a Certificate Template for Virtual Smart Cards
Exercise 6.3	Configuring a Domain Password Policy
Exercise 6.4	Configuring Account Lockout Settings
Exercise 6.5	Configuring a Password Settings Object
Exercise 6.6	Managing Windows Credentials
Lab Challenge	Joining a Device using Workplace Join

BEFORE YOU BEGIN

The lab environment consists of student workstations connected to a local area network, along with a server that functions as the domain controller for a domain called contoso.com. The computers required for this lab are listed in Table 6-1.

Table 6-1
Computers required for Lab 6

Computer	*Operating System*	*Computer Name*
Server	Windows Server 2012 R2	RWDC01
Server	Windows Server 2012 R2	Server02
Client	Windows Server 8	Win8B

In addition to the computers, you will also need the software listed in Table 6-2 to complete Lab 6.

Table 6-2
Software required for Lab 6

Software	Location
Lab 6 student worksheet	Lab06_worksheet.docx (provided by instructor)

Working with Lab Worksheets

Each lab in this manual requires that you answer questions, shoot screen shots, and perform other activities that you will document in a worksheet named for the lab, such as Lab06_worksheet.docx. You will find these worksheets on the book companion site. It is recommended that you use a USB flash drive to store your worksheets so you can submit them to your instructor for review. As you perform the exercises in each lab, open the appropriate worksheet file, fill in the required information, and then save the file to your flash drive.

SCENARIO

After completing this lab, you will be able to:

- Install and configure an enterprise Certificate Authority

- Request a digital certificate

- Create a certificate template for Virtual Smart Cards

- Configure a domain password policy

- Configure account lockout settings

- Configure a Password Settings Object

- Managing Windows Credentials

Estimated lab time: 120 minutes

Exercise 6.1	Requesting a Digital Certificate
Overview	In this exercise, you will install a Certificate Authority and then request a digital certificate from the Certificate Authority.
Mindset	For years, Windows has included a Certificate Authority that can be used to distribute digital certificates to clients. When combined with group policies, a certificate authority can automatically deploy certificates to all clients within the organization.
Completion time	30 minutes

First, you will install and configure a Certificate Authority by performing the following steps:

1. On *RWDC01*, log on using the **contoso\administrator** account and the **Pa$$w0rd** password.

2. Using *Server Manager*, click **Manage > Add Roles and Features**.

3. On the *Add Roles and Features Wizard* page, click **Next**.

4. On the *Select installation type* page, click **Next**.

5. On the *Select destination server* page, click **Next**.

6. On the *Select server roles* page, select **Active Directory Certificate Services**. On the *Add Roles and Features Wizard* page, click **Add Features** and then click **Next**.

7. On the *Select features* page, click **Next**.

8. On the *Active Directory Certificate Services* page, click **Next**.

9. On the *Select role services* page, ensure that the following is selected and then click **Next**.

   ● **Certification Authority**
   ● **Certificate Enrollment Policy Web Service**
   ● **Online Responder**

When you are prompted to add features, click **Add Features**.

10. On the *Web Server Role (IIS)* page, click **Next**.

11. On the *Select role services* page, click **Next**.

12. On the *Confirm installation selections* page, click **Install**.

13. On the *Installation progress* page, after the installation is successful, click **Configure Active Directory Certificate Services on the destination server**.

14. On the *Credentials* page, click **Next**.

15. On the *Select role services to configure* page, select the following and then click **Next**:

    ● **Certification Authority**
    ● **Online Responder**
    ● **Certificate Enrollment Policy Web Service**

16. On the *Setup Type* page, ensure that **Enterprise CA** is selected and then click **Next**.

17. On the *CA Type* page, ensure that **Root CA** is selected and then click **Next**.

18. On the *Private Key* page, ensure that *Create a new private key* is selected and then click **Next**.

19. On the *Cryptography for CA* page, answer the following question. Then change the *Key length* to **4096** and then click **Next**.

Question 1	*What is the default key length?*

20. On the *CA Name* page, answer the following question and then click **Next**.

Question 2	*What is the default CA name?*

21. On the *Validity Period* page, answer the following question. Then change the validity period to **10** years and click **Next**.

Question 3	*What is the default validity period?*

22. The *CA Database* page displays where the certificate database will be stored. Answer the following question and then click **Next**.

Question 4	*Where is the default database and log file location and why should caution be used here?*

23. On the *Authentication Type for CEP* page, click **Next**.

24. On the *Server Certificate* page, click to select the **Choose and assign a certificate for SSL later** and then click **Next**.

25. On the *Confirmation* page, click **Configure**.

26. Take a screen shot showing a successful configuration of the Active Directory Certificate Services by pressing **Alt+PrtScr** and then paste it into your Lab 6 worksheet file in the page provided by pressing **Ctrl+V**.

27. On the *Results* page, click **Close**.

28. If you are prompted to configure additional role services, click **Yes**.

29. Click **Close** to close the *Add Roles and Features Wizard*.

Next, you will request a certificate using the Certificate Console by performing the following steps:

1. Log on to *Win8B* as **contoso\administrator** with **Pa$$w0rd**, type **mmc** on the *Start* screen, and then click the **mmc** icon.

2. In the console, click **File > Add/Remove Snap-in**.

3. In the *Add or Remove Snap-ins* dialog box, double-click **Certificates**.

4. In the *Certificates snap-in* dialog box, click **My user account** and then click **Finish**.

5. Back in the *Add or Remove Snap-ins* dialog box, click **OK**.

6. Under the *Console Root*, expand **Certificates - Current** and then click **Personal** (see Figure 6-1).

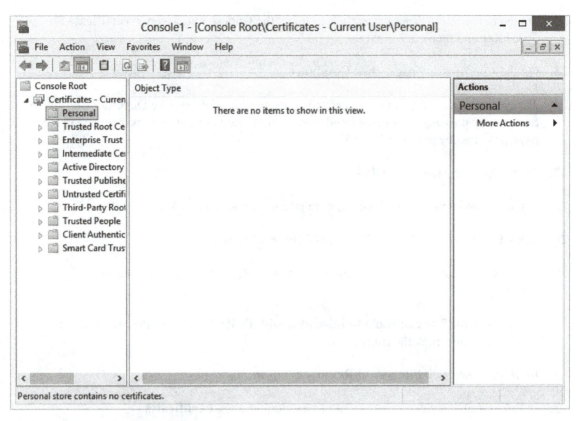

Figure 6-1
The Certificates Snap-in

7. Right-click **Personal** and choose **All Tasks > Request New Certificate**.

8. On the *Before You Begin* page, click **Next**.

9. On the *Select Certificate Enrollment Policy* page, click **Next**.

10. On the *Request Certificates* page, click to select the **User** certificate and then click **Enroll**.

11. When the certificate has been requested, click **Finish**.

12. Expand **Personal** and then click **Certificates**. You should see the *Administrator user* certificate. If you scroll over to the right, you should also see the *Intended Purpose*.

13. Take a screen shot showing a successful configuration of a Personal Certificate by pressing **Alt+PrtScr** and then paste it into your Lab 6 worksheet file in the page provided by pressing **Ctrl+V**.

End of exercise. Log out of Win8B.

Exercise 6.2	Creating a Certificate Template for Virtual Smart Cards
Overview	In this exercise, you will create a certificate template for virtual smart cards. Unfortunately, since our virtual environment does not have any mobile computers with TPMs, you will not be able to use these certificates.
Mindset	Microsoft developed virtual smart cards that emulate the functionality of traditional smart cards, without requiring the purchase of additional hardware such as smart card readers and related devices. Virtual smart cards (VMC) utilize the TPM chip that is usually included with most modern mobile computers. Since the TPM chip is tied to an individual computer, the user's possession of the computer is equivalent to the possession of a smart card.
Completion time	15 minutes

1. On *RWDC01*, log on using the **contoso\administrator** account and the **Pa$$w0rd** account.

2. Open **Microsoft Management Console (MMC)** by typing **mmc** from the *Start* menu.

3. Select **File > Add/Remove Snap-in**.

4. In the available snap-ins list, double-click **Certificate Templates**, and then click **OK**.

5. Double click **Certificate Templates** to view all available certificate templates.

6. Right-click the **Smartcard Logon template** and choose **Duplicate Template**.

7. On the *Compatibility* tab, under *Certification Authority*, click **Windows Server 2003**.

8. On the *General* tab, for the name, type **TPM Virtual Smart Card Logon**.

9. On the *Request Handling* tab, set the *Purpose* to **Signature and smartcard logon**. When you are prompted to confirm, click **Yes**. Then select **Prompt the user during enrollment**.

10. On the *Cryptography* tab, set the minimum key size to **2048**. Click to select **Requests must use one of the following providers**, and then select **Microsoft Base Smart Card Crypto Provider**.

11. On the *Security* tab, select **Authenticated Users**. Then select **Allow Enroll** and **Allow Autoenroll**.

Question 5	What permissions are required for a user to request a certificate?

12. Click **OK** to close the *Properties of New Template* dialog box.

13. Using *Server Manager*, click **Tools > Certificate Authority**.

14. In the left panel of the MMC, expand **Certification Authority (Local)**, and then expand your **contoso-RWDC01-CA-1** within the *Certification Authority* list.

15. Right-click **Certificate Templates** and choose **New > Certificate Template to Issue**.

16. From the list, select the **TPM Virtual Smart Card Logon**, and then click **OK**.

17. Take a screen shot showing a successful configuration of a certificate template by pressing **Alt+PrtScr** and then paste it into your Lab 6 worksheet file in the page provided by pressing **Ctrl+V**.

Exercise 6.3	Configuring a Domain Password Policy
Overview	In this exercise, you will define a domain-level password policy including maximum password length and password history.
Mindset	You can define only account policies, which include password policy, account lockout policy, and Kerberos policy, at the domain level. Because most organizations will have only one domain, you can set only one.
Completion time	10 minutes

1. On *RWDC01*, using *Server Manager*, click **Tools > Group Policy Management**. The *Group Policy Management* console opens.

2. Navigate to and right-click **Default Domain Policy** and choose **Edit**. The *Group Policy Management Editor* opens.

3. In the left window pane, expand the **Computer Configuration** node, expand the **Policies** node, and expand the **Windows Settings** folder. Then expand the **Security Settings** node. In the *Security Settings* node, expand **Account Policies** and select **Password Policy**, as shown in Figure 6-2.

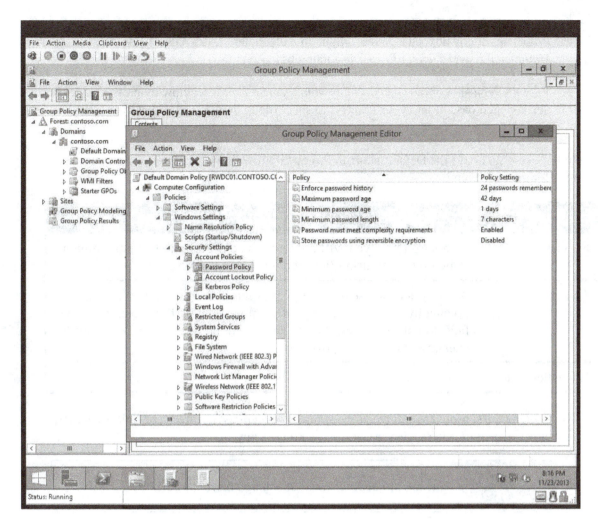

Figure 6-2
Managing Password Policy

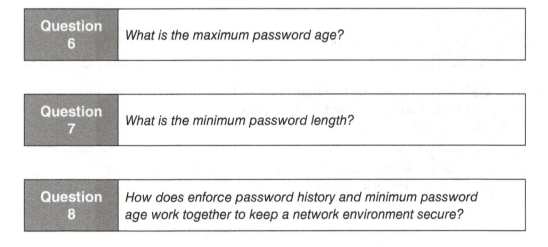

| Question 6 | What is the maximum password age? |

| Question 7 | What is the minimum password length? |

| Question 8 | How does enforce password history and minimum password age work together to keep a network environment secure? |

4. Double-click the **Minimum password length**. In the *Minimum password length Properties* dialog box, change the 7 value to 8 characters. Click **OK** to close the *Minimum password length Properties* dialog box.

5. Take a screen shot of the *Group Policy Management Editor* window by pressing **Alt+Prt Scr** and then paste it into your Lab 6 worksheet file in the page provided by pressing **Ctrl+V**.

End of exercise. Leave the Default Domain Policy Group Policy Management Editor window open for the next exercise.

Exercise 6.4	Configuring Account Lockout Settings
Overview	In this exercise, you will continue to configure the Default Domain Policy by configuring the account lockout settings.
Mindset	Account lockout settings help prevent a user from hacking into an account by continually trying different passwords. Therefore, if a hacker fails too many times, the account will be locked, and any further attempts will be not be possible.
Completion time	10 minutes

1. On *RWDC01*, using *Default Domain Policy Group Policy Management Editor* console, under *Account Policies*, click **Account Lockout Policy**.

Question 9	How are the account lockout settings currently set?

2. Double-click **Account lockout duration**. In the *Account lockout duration Properties* dialog box, click to enable the **Define this policy** setting.

Question 10	What is the default value for the Account lockout duration?

3. Click **OK** to close the *Account lockout duration Properties* dialog box. In the *Suggested Value Changes* dialog box, look at the suggested settings and then click **OK**.

Question 11	How many invalid logon attempts can be made that will cause an account to be locked?

4. Take a screen shot of the *Account Lockout Policy* window by pressing **Alt+Prt Scr** and then paste it into your Lab 6 worksheet file in the page provided by pressing **Ctrl+V**.

5. Close the *Group Policy Management Editor* window for the Default Domain Policy.

6. Close the *Group Policy Management* console.

End of exercise. Remain logged in for the next exercise.

Exercise 6.5	Configuring a Password Settings Object
Overview	In this exercise, you will create and apply a Password Settings Object to the Sales group.
Mindset	Password Settings Objects (PSOs) are created and assigned to user objects or global security groups. These settings will overwrite the domain level settings for security settings, including the password policies and account lockout settings.
Completion time	30 minutes

1. On *RWDC01*, using *Server Manager*, click **Tools > Active Directory Users and Computers**. The *Active Directory Users and Computers* console opens.

2. Right-click **contoso.com** and choose **New > Organizational Unit**.

3. When the *New Object – Organizational Unit* dialog box opens, type **Sales** in the *Name* text box. Click **OK** to close the *New Object – Organizational Unit* dialog box.

4. Right-click the **Sales** organizational unit and choose **New > User**. The *New Object – User* dialog box opens.

5. Type the following information and then click **Next**:

   First name: **John**

   Last name: **Smith**

   User logon name: **JSmith**

6. For the *Password* and *Confirm password* text boxes, type **Pa$$w0rd**.

7. Click to select **Password never expires**. When the warning appears, click **OK**. Click **Next**.

8. Click **Finish**.

9. Create a user in the Sales OU with the following information:

   First name: **Stacy**

   Last name: **Jones**

   User logon name: **SJones**

   Password: **Pa$$w0rd**

   Select **Password never expires**

10. Click **Finish** to close the *New Object – User* dialog box.

11. Right-click the **Sales OU** and choose **New > Group**. The *New Object – Group* dialog box opens.

12. In the *Group name* text box, type **Sales** and then click **OK**.

13. Double-click the **Sales** group. The *Sales Properties* dialog box opens.

14. Click the **Members** tab.

15. Click **Add**. The *Select Users, Contacts, Computers, Service Accounts, or Groups* dialog box opens.

16. In the text box, type **John Smith; Stacy Jones** and then click **OK**.

17. Take a screen shot of the *Sales Properties* dialog box window by pressing **Alt+PrtScr** and then paste it into your Lab 6 worksheet file in the page provided by pressing **Ctrl+V**.

18. Click **OK** to close the *Sales Properties* dialog box.

19. On *RWDC01*, using *Server Manager*, click **Tools > Active Directory Administrative Center**. The Active Directory Administrative Center opens.

20. In the Active Directory Administrative Center navigation pane, click the arrow next to the *contoso (local)* and then select the **System** folder. Scroll down and double-click **Password Settings Container**. The *Password Settings Container* is shown in Figure 6-3.

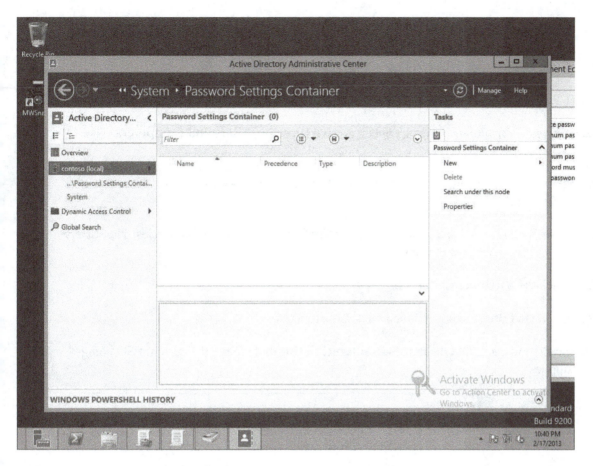

Figure 6-3
Managing Password Settings Container

21. In the *Tasks* pane, click **New > Password Settings**. The *Create Password Settings* window opens.

22. In the *Name* text box, type **PSO1**.

23. In the *Precedence* text box, type **1**.

24. Change the minimum password length to **12**.

25. Click to enable **Enforce account lockout policy**.

26. Set the *Number of failed logon attempts* to **3**.

27. Change both the *Reset failed logon attempts count after* and *Account will be locked out for a duration of* to **15** minutes.

28. In the *Directly Applies To* section, click the **Add** button.

29. In the *Select Users or Groups* dialog box, type **Sales** in the text box and then click **OK**.

30. Click **OK** to submit the creation of the PSO.

31. Close the **Active Directory Administrative Center**.

32. Using *Server Manager*, open **Tools > Active Directory Users and Computers**. The *Active Directory Users and Computers* console opens.

33. Click the **View** menu and make sure that *Advanced Features* is checked. If it is not, click **Advanced Features**.

34. Open the **Sales** OU and then right-click **John Smith** and choose **Properties**. The *<user> Properties* dialog box opens.

35. Click the **Attribute Editor** tab.

36. Click the **Filter** button, and then click **Constructed**.

37. Scroll down and find the **msDS-ResultantPSO** attribute to see the current PSO being applied.

Question 12	Which PSO is applied?

38. Take a screen shot of the *Attribute Editor* tab by pressing **Alt+PrtScr** and then paste it into your Lab 6 worksheet file in the page provided by pressing **Ctrl+V**.

39. Click **OK** to close John Smith Properties dialog box.

40. Close the **Active Directory Users and Computers** console.

End of exercise. Remain logged in for the next exercise.

Exercise 6.6	Managing Windows Credentials
Overview	In this exercise, you will use some of the new tools in Windows 8.1 to manage the credentials for the users you have created.
Mindset	Windows 8.1 provides support for a number of alternative authentication methods, including PINs, Smart Cards, biometrics, and picture passwords.
Completion time	10 minutes

1. On *Win8B*, right-click the **Start** button and choose **Control Panel**. The *Control Panel* appears.

2. Click **User Accounts > Credential Manager**. The *Credential Manager* control panel applet appears, as shown in Figure 6-4.

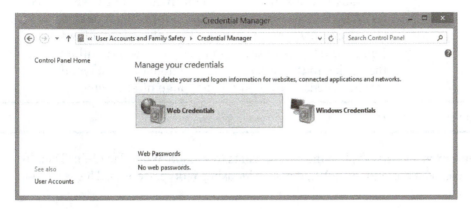

Figure 6-4
The Credential Manager control panel

3. Click **Windows Credentials** and then click **Add a Windows credential**. The *Add a Windows Credential* dialog box appears.

4. In the *Internet or network address* text box, type **\\RemotePC**.

5. In the *User name* text box, type **Administrator**.

6. In the *Password* text box, type **Pa$$w0rd** and then click **OK**. The credential appears in the *Windows Credentials* list. Now, any time that you access the \\RemotePC, you will use the username administrator with the password of Pa$$w0rd.

7. Take a screen shot of the *Windows Credentials* control panel showing the new credential you entered by pressing **Ctrl+PrtScr** and then paste the resulting image into the Lab 6 worksheet file in the page provided by pressing **Ctrl+V**.

End of exercise. Close all windows.

Lab Challenge	Joining a Device using Workplace Join
Overview	In this exercise, you will explain how to join a device using Workplace Join.
Mindset	As many organizations implement Bring Your Own Device (BYOD) policies, users will use their personal devices to access organization resources. Workplace Join allows users to join their devices to the organization network, without joining the device to the Active Directory domain. You can then manage access based on a wide range of attributes.
Completion time	15 minutes

During this exercise, first explain the requirements to support Workplace Join. Then list the steps you would use to join a Windows tablet using Workplace Join. This is a written exercise only.

End of lab.

LAB 7
SUPPORTING DATA STORAGE

THIS LAB CONTAINS THE FOLLOWING EXERCISES AND ACTIVITIES:

Exercise 7.1   Enabling Disk Quotas on Windows 8.1

Exercise 7.2   Creating a Storage Pool and a Storage Space

Exercise 7.3   Installing and Configuring BranchCache on a File Server

Exercise 7.4   Using OneDrive to Manage Files and Folders

Lab Challenge   Creating a DFS Namespace

BEFORE YOU BEGIN

The lab environment consists of student workstations connected to a local area network, along with a server that functions as the domain controller for a domain called contoso.com. The computers required for this lab are listed in Table 7-1.

Table 7-1
Computers Required for Lab 7

Computer	Operating System	Computer Name
Server	Windows Server 2012 R2	RWDC01
Server	Windows Server 2012 R2	Server02
Client	Windows 8.1	Win8B

In addition to the computers, you will also need the software listed in Table 7-2 to complete Lab 7.

Table 7-2
Software Required for Lab 7

Software	Location
Lab 7 student worksheet	Lab07_worksheet.docx (provided by instructor)

Working with Lab Worksheets

Each lab in this manual requires that you answer questions, shoot screen shots, and perform other activities that you will document in a worksheet named for the lab, such as Lab07_worksheet.docx. You will find these worksheets on the book companion site. It is recommended that you use a USB flash drive to store your worksheets so you can submit them to your instructor for review. As you perform the exercises in each lab, open the appropriate worksheet file, fill in the required information, and then save the file to your flash drive.

SCENARIO

After completing this lab, you will be able to:

- Enable disk quotas on a computer running Windows 8.1

- Create a storage pool and a storage space on Windows 8.1

- Install and configure BranchCache

- Use OneDrive to manage files and folders

Estimated lab time: 110 minutes

Exercise 7.1	Enabling Disk Quotas on Windows 8.1
Overview	In this exercise, you will create disk quotas on Windows 8 that will limit how much disk space a user can use on a computer.
Mindset	To prevent users from filling up the C drive or other data drives, you can use Disk Quotas.
Completion time	10 minutes

1. On *Win8B*, log on using the **contoso\administrator** account and the **Pa$$word** password.

2. Click the **Desktop** tile.

3. Right-click the **Start** menu and choose **Disk Management**.

4. If you are prompted to initialize any disks, click **OK** to initialize the disks.

5. Right-click the **C** drive and choose **Properties**.

6. Click the **Quota** tab (see Figure 7-1) and then click **Enable Quota management**.

Figure 7-1
The Quota tab

7. Select **Limit disk space to** and then type **500** in the field provided. Click the down arrow and select **MB**.

8. For the *Set warning level to* setting, type **300** in the field provided. Click the down arrow and select **MB**.

9. In the *Select the quota logging options for this volume* section, select both **Log event when a user exceeds their quota limit** and **Log event when a user exceeds their warning level**.

10. Click **OK**.

11. After reading the disk quota message, click **OK**.

12. Right-click the **C** drive and choose **Properties**.

13. Click the **Quota** tab and then choose **Quota Entries** to see whether any user accounts are currently reaching their limits.

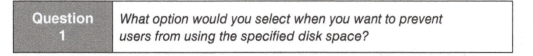

Question 1	What option would you select when you want to prevent users from using the specified disk space?

14. Take a screen shot of the *Quota Entries* dialog box by pressing **Alt+PrtScr** and then paste it into your Lab 7 worksheet file in the page provided by pressing **Ctrl+V**.

15. Close the *Quota Entries* window, close the *Local Disk (C:) Properties* dialog box, and then close **Disk Management**.

End of exercise. Close any open windows before you begin the next exercise.

Exercise 7.2	Creating a Storage Pool and a Storage Space
Overview	In this exercise, you will create a storage pool and then you will create a storage space on a computer running Windows 8.1.
Mindset	To improve the performance and reliability of the disk system used on Windows 8.1, you can use Storage Pool and Storage Space to use disk space from multiple disks.
Completion time	10 minutes

1. On *Win8B*, right-click the **Start** button and choose **Control Panel**.

2. In the *Control Panel* pane, click **System and Security > Storage Spaces**.

3. On the *Manage Storage Spaces* page (see Figure 7-2), click **Create a new pool and storage space**.

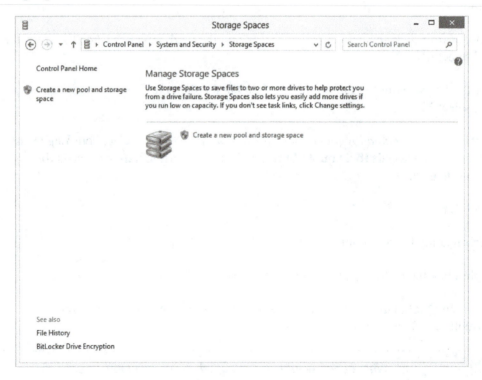

Figure 7-2
The Manage Storage Spaces page

4. On the *Select drives to create a storage pool* page, click **Create pool**.

Question 2	Which drive letter will be assigned to the Storage space?

Question 3	What is the default resiliency type?

Question 4	How many disk failures can a two-way mirror have before you lose the data?

5. Click the **Create storage space** button.

6. Take a screen shot showing the *Manage Storage Spaces* page by pressing **Alt+PrtScr** and then paste it into your Lab 7 worksheet file in the page provided by pressing **Ctrl+V**.

End of exercise. Close any open windows before you begin the next exercise.

Exercise 7.3	Installing and Configuring BranchCache on a File Server
Overview	In this exercise, you will install and configure BranchCache so that it can be used with file shares.
Mindset	BranchCache allows for WAN acceleration functionality by using multiple systems to create a cache infrastructure, which is used to increase performance of web sites and shared folders.
Completion time	30 minutes

1. On *Server02*, log on using the **contoso\administrator** account and the **Pa$$w0rd** password.

2. On *Server02*, using *Server Manager*, click **Manage > Add Roles and Features**. The *Add Roles and Features Wizard* opens.

3. Click **Next**.

4. On the *Select Installation Type* page, ensure that **Role-based or feature-based installation** is selected and then click **Next**.

5. On the *Select destination server* page, click **Server02.contoso.com** and then click **Next**.

6. On the *Select server roles* page, under *Roles*, expand **File and Storage Services** and then expand **File and iSCSI Services**. Click to select **BranchCache for Network Files** and then click **Next**.

7. On the *Select features* page, click **Next**.

8. On the *Confirm installation selections* page, click **Install**. When installation is complete, click **Close**.

9. On *RWDC01*, log on using the **contoso\administrator** account and the **Pa$$w0rd** password.

10. On *RWDC01*, using *Server Manager*, click **Tools > Active Directory Users and Computers**.

11. In the *Active Directory Users and Computers* console, right-click **CONTOSO.COM** and choose **New > Organizational Unit**.

12. In the *New Object – Organization Unit* dialog box, in the *Name* text box, type **Servers** and then click **OK**.

13. Close **Active Directory Users and Computers**.

14. On *RWDC01*, using *Server Manager*, click **Tools > Group Policy Management**. The Group Policy Management console opens.

15. Navigate to and right-click the **Servers** OU and then choose **Create a GPO in this domain, and Link it here**.

16. In the *New GPO* dialog box, in the *Name* text box, type **BranchCache for Servers**.

17. Click **OK** to close the *New GPO* dialog box.

18. Expand the **Servers** OU and then right-click the **BranchCache for Servers** GPO and choose **Edit**.

19. In the *Group Policy Management Editor* window, expand the following path: **Computer Configuration > Policies > Administrative Templates > Network**. Under *Network*, click **Lanman Server** (see Figure 7-3).

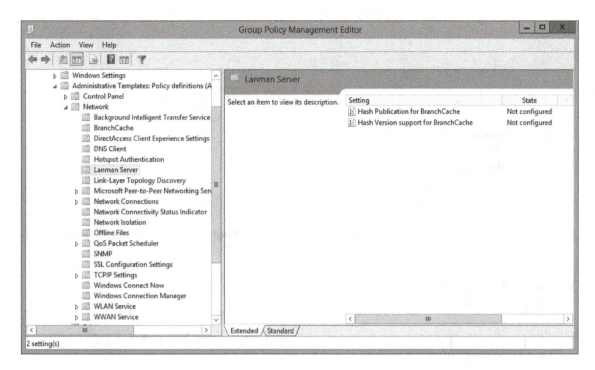

Figure 7-3
The Lanman Server node in a GPO

Question 5	*What must all servers in a BranchCache infrastructure have?*

20. Double-click **Hash Publication for BranchCache**. The *Hash Publication for BranchCache* dialog box opens.

21. In the *Hash Publication for BranchCache* dialog box, click **Enabled**.

22. In the *Options* section, **Allow hash publication for all shared folders** is already selected.

23. Take a screen shot of the *Hash Publication for BranchCache* dialog box by pressing **Alt+PrtScr** and then paste it into your Lab 7 worksheet file in the page provided by pressing **Ctrl+V**.

24. Click **OK** to close the *Hash Publication for BranchCache* dialog box.

25. Close **Group Policy Management Editor**.

26. On *Server02*, open *File Explorer* by clicking the **File Explorer** icon on the taskbar.

27. Expand **This PC**, right-click **Local Disk (C:)** and choose **New > Folder**. Name the folder **SharedFolder** and then press **Enter**.

28. Right-click the **C:\SharedFolder** and choose **Properties**.

29. Click the **Sharing** tab.

30. Click **Advanced Sharing**.

31. Click **Share this folder** and then click **OK** to close the *Advanced Sharing* dialog box.

32. Click **Close** to close the *SharedFolder Properties* dialog box.

33. Close **File Explorer**.

34. On *Server02*, using *Server Manager*, click **Tools > Computer Management**.

35. In the *Computer Management* console, under **System Tools**, expand **Shared Folders** and then click **Shares**.

36. In the *Details* pane, right-click **SharedFolder** and choose **Properties**. The share's *Properties* dialog box opens.

37. In the *Properties* dialog box, on the *General* tab, click **Offline Settings**. The *Offline Settings* dialog box opens.

38. Ensure that **Only the files and programs that users specify are available offline** is selected and then click to select **Enable BranchCache**.

39. Take a screen shot of the *Offline Settings* dialog box by pressing **Alt+PrtScr** and then paste it into your Lab 7 worksheet file in the page provided by pressing **Ctrl+V**.

40. Click **OK** twice.

41. Close **Computer Management**.

42. On *RWDC01*, using *Group Policy Management*, expand **Group Policy Objects**, and then right-click **BranchCache for Servers** and choose **Edit**.

43. In the *Group Policy Management Editor* window, navigate to the **Computer Configuration > Policies > Administrative Templates > Network** node, and then click **BranchCache**.

44. Double-click **Set BranchCache Distributed Cache mode**.

45. In the **Set BranchCache Distributed Cache mode** dialog box, click **Enabled**.

46. Click **OK** to close the *Set BranchCache Distributed Cache* mode.

47. Close **Group Policy Management Editor**.

48. Close **Group Policy Management**.

End of exercise. Close any open windows before you begin the next exercise.

Exercise 7.4	Using OneDrive to Manage Files and Folders
Overview	In this exercise, you will connect to the Internet to access OneDrive to create and manage Office documents. Unlike the other exercises you have completed thus far, you will perform this exercise on a client computer that has access to the Internet.
Mindset	OneDrive, formerly called SkyDrive, allows users to create and store documents in the cloud.
Completion time	35 minutes

> **NOTE**
>
> *OneDrive is a cloud-based service that is offered by Microsoft over the Internet. Therefore, to use OneDrive, you need to use a computer running Windows 8 with Internet access.*
>
> *For example, you may use one of the following two computer options:*
>
> - *A Windows Server 2012 with Hyper-V computer that has Internet access, running a Windows 8.1 virtual machine.*
>
> - *A Windows 8.1 computer with Internet access. You will also need to have administrative access to this computer.*

First, create a OneDrive account and file by performing the following steps:

1. On the classroom computer that has Internet access, open **Internet Explorer** and go to the **http://onedrive.live.com** website. At the top of the IE window, click **Sign Up**.

2. At the bottom of the screen, click **Sign up now**.

3. On the *Microsoft account* page, in the *Name* section, type your **First** name and then type your **Last** name.

4. In the *How would you like to sign in?* section, click the **Or get a new email address** link and then type the following email address:

   Microsoft account name: **<FirstName>.<LastName>.Training.<Month>-<Year>@outlook.com.**

   Therefore, if your name is *John Smith*, and you are performing this lab in June 2014, you would type:

   John.Smith.Training.06-2014@outlook.com

Question 6	*What is the email address?*

5. In the *Create a password* text box and the *Reenter password* text box, type **Pa$$w0rd**.

6. In the *ZIP code* text box, type your ZIP code.

7. For the *Birthdate* section, click the down arrows to choose your **Month, Day** and **Year**.

8. In the *Gender* section, click the down arrow to **Select one** (a gender).

9. In the *Phone number* text box, type your phone number.

10. In the *Alternate email address* text box, type a personal email address.

11. In the *We want to make sure that a real person is creating an account* text box, type the character string that is shown in the empty text box.

12. Click to deselect the **Send me promotional offers from Microsoft** option.

13. Click **Create account**.

14. After the OneDrive account is created, press **Ctrl+PrtScr** to take a screen shot. Press **Ctrl+V** to paste the image on the page provided in the Lab 7 worksheet file.

15. Click the **Documents** folder.

16. From the menu at the top of the page, click **Create > Folder**.

17. Name the folder **Project Files** and click **Create**. Then click the folder to open it.

18. From the menu at the top of the page, click **Create > Word document**.

19. When the web version of Outlook is loaded, type your first name and last name in the document.

20. At the top of the screen, click **Document1**. Then type **ProjectScope** and press **Enter**.

21. Type a few words in the document. Notice that there is no save button since the document is automatically saved.

22. Click the **OneDrive** link (located at the upper-left corner) to return to the main screen.

23. Open the **Documents** folder and then open the **Project Files** folder.

24. Press **Ctrl+PrtScr** to take a screen shot of the *Project Files* folder showing the *ProjectScope* document. Press **Ctrl+V** to paste the image on the page provided in the Lab 7 worksheet file.

25. Close **Internet Explorer**.

26. On the workstation, right-click the **Start** button and choose **Computer Management**.

27. When the *Computer Management* console opens, expand **Local Users and Groups**, and then click **Users**.

28. Right-click **Users**, and click **New User**.

29. When the *User name* dialog box opens, type the following information and then click **Create**.

    User name: **SMason**

    Full name: **Simon Mason**

    Password and Confirm password: **Pa$$w0rd**

    Deselect **User must change password at next logon**

30. Click **Close** to close the *New User* dialog box.

31. Log off as administrator, and then log on as **win8b\SMason** with the **Pa$$w0rd** password.

NOTE	In several of the following steps, you'll see reference to onscreen options titled "SkyDrive". At the time of publication, the software continued to use "SkyDrive" for these onscreen option names. These names will change to "OneDrive" in future versions of the software.

32. From the *Start* menu, click the **SkyDrive** tile.

33. Click **Go to PC settings**.

34. Click **Connect to a Microsoft account**.

35. On the *Switch to a Microsoft account on this PC* page, type **Pa$$w0rd** in the *Current password* text box and then click **Next**.

36. On the *Sign into your Microsoft account* page, type the username that you recorded in Question 6 and the password of **Pa$$w0rd**. Click **Next**.

37. On the *Help us protect your info* page, select the **Email** option so that you can retrieve a security code. Then type the entire email address and click **Next**.

38. After you retrieve the code from your email address, type the code in the *Code* text box and then click **Next**.

39. On the *SkyDrive is your cloud storage* page, click **Next**. Then click **Switch**.

40. Press **Alt+F4** to go back to the *Start* menu. Then click the **Sky Drive** tile.

41. On the *SkyDrive* page, click **Documents**, and then click **Project Files**.

42. Press **Ctrl+PrtScr** to take a screen shot of the *Project Files* folder. Press **Ctrl+V** to paste the image on the page provided in the Lab 7 worksheet file.

End of exercise. Close any open windows before you begin the next exercise.

Lab Challenge	Creating a DFS Namespace
Overview	To complete this challenge, you must install a DFS Namespace, then create a DFS Namespace that groups \\server02\share and \\server03\share.
Mindset	DFS Namespace can be used to organize multiple shared folders into a shared folder infrastructure. By accessing the DFS Namespace, users do not worry about which server hosts the shared folders. Instead, the users click and go the specific shared folder.
Completion time	25 minutes

Write the steps you would take to cache web traffic from Server02.

End of lab.

LAB 8
MANAGING DATA SECURITY

THIS LAB CONTAINS THE FOLLOWING EXERCISES AND ACTIVITIES:

Exercise 8.1	Managing NTFS and Share Permissions
Exercise 8.2	Encrypting Files with Encrypting File System (EFS)
Exercise 8.3	Encrypting a Volume with BitLocker
Exercise 8.4	Using Dynamic Access Control (DAC)
Lab Challenge	Using BitLocker To Go

BEFORE YOU BEGIN

The lab environment consists of student workstations connected to a local area network, along with a server that functions as the domain controller for a domain called contoso.com. The computers required for this lab are listed in Table 8-1.

Table 8-1
Computers Required for Lab 8

Computer	Operating System	Computer Name
Server	Windows Server 2012 R2	RWDC01
Server	Windows Server 2012 R2	Server02
Client	Windows 8.1	Win8A
Client	Windows 8.1	Win8B

In addition to the computers, you will also need the software listed in Table 8-2 to complete Lab 8.

Table 8-2
Software Required for Lab 8

Software	Location
Lab 8 student worksheet	Lab08_worksheet.docx (provided by instructor)

Working with Lab Worksheets

Each lab in this manual requires that you answer questions, shoot screen shots, and perform other activities that you will document in a worksheet named for the lab, such as Lab08_worksheet.docx. You will find these worksheets on the book companion site. It is recommended that you use a USB flash drive to store your worksheets so you can submit them to your instructor for review. As you perform the exercises in each lab, open the appropriate worksheet file, fill in the required information, and then save the file to your flash drive.

SCENARIO

After completing this lab, you will be able to:

- Manage NTFS and share permissions

- Encrypt a file with EFS

- Encrypt a volume with BitLocker

- Use Dynamic Access Control

- Use BitLocker to Go

Estimated lab time: 140 minutes

Exercise 8.1	Managing NTFS and Share Permissions
Overview	In this exercise, you will create a folder, share the folder, and then configure the NTFS and share permissions.
Mindset	As a Windows administrator, you need to know how to manage files and folders, including how to configure NTFS and share permissions so that users can access the files that they need in order to perform their job while preventing other users from accessing the same files.
Completion time	20 minutes

1. On *RWDC01*, log on using the **contoso\administrator** account and the **Pa$$w0rd** password.

2. Using *Server Manager*, click **Tools > Active Directory Users and Computers**.

3. Right-click the **Users** OU and choose **New > User**.

4. For the *First name* text box and the *User logon name* text box, type **User2**. Click **Next**.

5. For the *Password* text box and the *Confirm password* text box, type **Pa$$w0rd**. Click to deselect **User must change password at next logon** and then select **Password never expires**. Click **Next**.

6. Click **Finish**.

7. Close **Active Directory Users and Computers**.

8. On *Win8A*, log on using the **contoso\administrator** account and the **Pa$$w0rd** password.

9. Click the **Desktop** tile.

10. On the taskbar, click the **File Explorer** icon to open *File Explorer*.

11. Under *This PC*, click **Local Disk (C:)**. Then right-click, **Local Disk (C:)** and choose **New > Folder**. For the folder name, type **Data**, and press the Enter key.

12. Right-click the **Data** folder and choose **Properties**.

13. Click the **Sharing** tab.

14. Click the **Advanced Sharing** button.

15. Click to select **Share this folder**.

16. To configure the share permissions, click the **Permissions** button.

17. With *Everyone* already selected, click to select **Allow Full Control**.

18. Click **OK** to close the *Permission for Data* dialog box.

19. Click **OK** to close the *Advanced Sharing* dialog box.

20. To manage the NTFS permissions, click the **Security** tab.

Question 1	Which permissions do Authenticated Users have?

21. Click the **Advanced** button.

22. In the *Advanced Security Settings for Data* dialog box (see Figure 8-1), click the **Effective Access** tab.

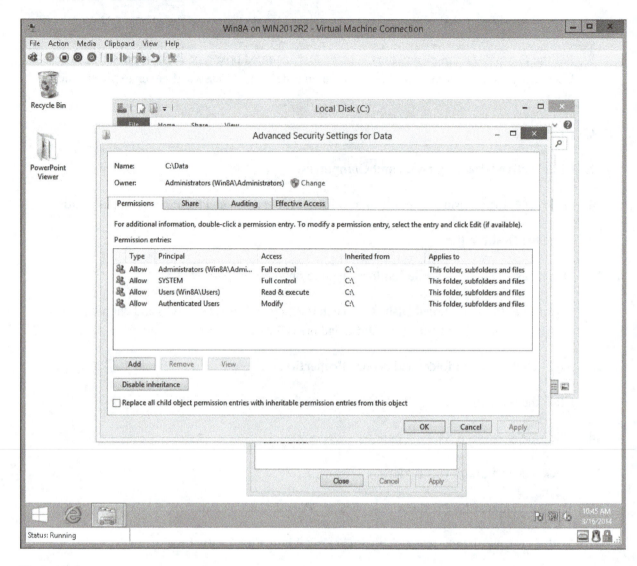

Figure 8-1
The *Advanced Security Settings for Data* dialog box

23. Click **Select a user**.

24. In the *Select Users, Computers, Service Accounts, or Groups* dialog box, in the *Enter the object name to select* text box, type **User2** and then click **OK**.

25. Click the **View effective access** button.

> | **Question 2** | *Which permission does User2 not have for the Data folder?* |

26. Click **OK** to close the *Advanced Security Settings for Data* dialog box.

27. Click the **Edit** button.

28. In the *Permissions for Data* dialog box, click **Add**.

29. In the *Select Users, Computers, Service Accounts, or Groups* dialog box, in the *Enter the object name to select* text box, type **User2** and then click **OK**.

30. With **User2** selected, click to select **Allow Full control**.

31. Click **OK** to close the *Permissions for Data* dialog box.

32. In the *Data Properties* dialog box, click the **Advanced** button.

33. Click the **Effective Access** tab.

34. Click **Select a user**.

35. In the *Select Users, Computers, Service Accounts, or Groups* dialog box, in the *Enter the object name to select* text box, type **User2** and then click **OK**.

36. Click the **View effective access** button.

Question 3	Which permission does User2 not have for the Data folder?

37. Take a screen shot of the *Advanced Security Settings for Data* dialog box by pressing **Alt+PrtScr** and then paste it into your Lab 8 worksheet file in the page provided by pressing **Ctrl+V**.

38. Click **OK** to close the *Advanced Security Settings for Data* dialog box.

39. Click **Close** to close the *Data Properties* dialog box.

End of exercise. Close all windows on Win8A.

Exercise 8.2	Encrypting Files with Encrypting File System (EFS)
Overview	For files that are extremely sensitive, you can use EFS to encrypt the files. In this exercise, you will encrypt a file using Encrypting File System (EFS), which is a built-in feature of NTFS.
Mindset	Encryption adds an additional level of security. As an example, by using encryption, you can ensure that if a laptop is stolen and the laptop's hard drive is put into another system where the thief or hacker is an administrator, the thief would not be able to read the files without using the proper key. If you want to encrypt individual documents, you can use Encrypting File System (EFS).
Completion time	50 minutes

First, you will encrypt files with EFS by performing the following steps:

1. On *Win8B*, log on using the **contoso\administrator** account with the **Pa$$w0rd** password. Click the **Desktop** tile.

2. On the taskbar, click the **File Explorer** icon to open *File Explorer*.

3. Click **This PC** and then double-click **Local Disk (C:)**.

4. Right-click the white space of the **Local Disk (C:)** window and choose **New > Folder**. For the folder name, type **Data** and then press **Enter**.

5. Double-click the **Data** folder.

6. Right-click the white space of the **Data** folder and choose **New > Text Document**. For the document name, type **Test** and press **Enter**.

7. Go back to the **C:** folder. Then right-click the **C:\Data** folder and choose **Properties**. The *Properties* dialog box opens.

8. On the **General** tab, click **Advanced**. The *Advanced Attributes* dialog box appears.

9. Click to select **Encrypt contents to secure data** and then click **OK**.

10. Click **OK** to close the *Data Properties* dialog box.

11. When you are prompted to confirm the changes, click **OK**.

Question 4	Which color is the C:\Data folder and what does the color indicate?

Question 5	Is the test.txt file in the C:\Data folder also encrypted?

12. Take a screen shot of the *Data* folder window by pressing **Alt+PrtScr** and then paste it into your Lab 8 worksheet file in the page provided by pressing **Ctrl+V**.

13. Right-click the **C:\Data** folder and choose **Properties**. The *Properties* dialog box opens.

14. On the **General** tab, click **Advanced**. The *Advanced Attributes* dialog box appears.

15. Click to deselect the **Encrypt contents to secure data** checkbox. Click **OK** to close the *Advanced Attributes* dialog box.

16. Click **OK** to close the *Data Properties* dialog box.

17. When you are prompted to confirm attribute changes, click **OK**.

18. On *Win8B*, log off as administrator.

Next, you will share files protected by EFS with other users by performing the following steps:

1. On *Win8B*, log on using the **contoso\User2** account and the **Pa$$w0rd** password.

2. After new user login set up, click the **Desktop** tile and then, on the taskbar, click the **File Explorer** icon.

3. Open the **C:\Data** folder, and then right-click the **test.txt** file and choose **Properties**.

4. On the **General** tab, click **Advanced**. The *Advanced Attributes* dialog box opens.

5. Click **Encrypt contents to secure data**. Click **OK** to close the *Advanced Attributes* dialog box. Click **OK** to close the *Test Properties* dialog box.

6. When you are prompted to encrypt the file and its parent folder, click **OK**.

7. On *Win8B*, log out as **User2** and log in using the **contoso\administrator** account and the **Pa$$w0rd** password.

8. Click the **Desktop** tile, open **File Explorer**, and then open the **C:\Data** folder.

9. Double-click to open the **test.txt** file.

Question 6	Which error message is displayed?

10. Click **OK** to close the message and then close **Notepad**.

11. Right-click the **test.txt** file and choose **Properties**.

12. Click the **Security** tab.

Question 7	Which permissions does the Administrator have?

Question 8	Why was the contoso\administrator unable to open the file?

13. Click the **General** tab, click the **Advanced** button, click to deselect the **Encrypt** check box, and then click **OK**.

14. Click **OK** to close the *Test Properties* dialog box. When the *Access Denied* dialog box appears, click **Cancel** to close it. If a UAC prompts you to continue to complete this operation, click **Continue**.

Question 9	Were you able to decrypt the file?

15. On *Win8B*, log off as Administrator and log using the **User2** account and the **Pa$$w0rd** password.

16. Click the **Desktop** tile, open **File Explo**rer, and then open the **C:** folder.

17. Right-click the **C:\Data** folder and choose **Properties**. The *Properties* dialog box appears.

18. Click the **Advanced** button. The *Advanced Attributes* dialog box appears.

19. Click to deselect the **Encrypt contents to secure data** checkbox and then click **OK**.

20. Click **OK** to close the Data *Properties* dialog box. When you are prompted to apply changes to the folder and its content, click **OK**. If you are prompted to confirm that you would like to continue, click **Continue**.

21. Log off as **User2** and logon using the **contoso\administrator** account and the **Pa$$word** password.

22. Click the **Desktop** tile, open **File Explorer**, and then open the **C:\Data** folder.

23. Right-click the **test.txt** file and choose **Properties**.

24. Click the **Advanced** button. The *Advanced Attributes* dialog box appears.

25. Click to select the **Encrypt contents to secure data** check box and then click **OK**.

26. Click **OK** to close the Test *Properties* dialog box. When you are prompted to apply changes to the folder and its contents, click **OK**.

27. Right-click the **test.txt** file and choose **Properties**.

28. Click the **Advanced** button. The *Advanced Attributes* dialog box appears.

29. Click the **Details** buttons. The *User Access to Test* dialog box appears (see Figure 8-2).

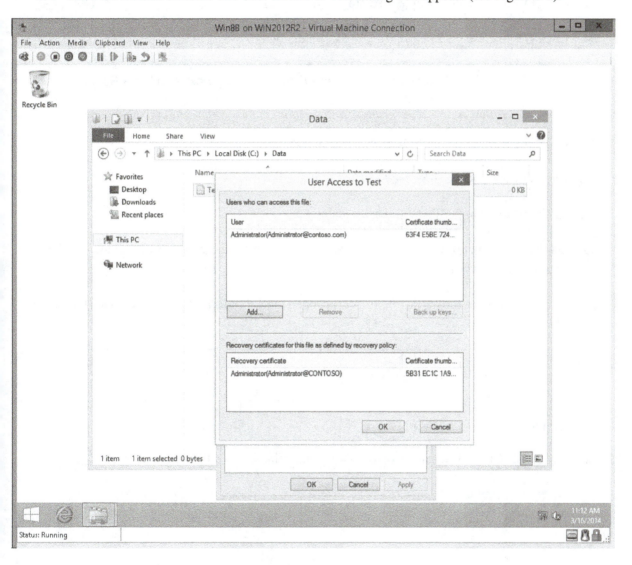

Figure 8-2
The *User Access to Test* dialog box

30. Click the **Add** button. In the *Encrypting File System* dialog box, click **User2**, and then click **View Certificate**.

31. Take a screen shot of the *Certificate* dialog box by pressing **Alt+PrtScr** and then paste it into your Lab 8 worksheet file in the page provided by pressing **Ctrl+V**.

32. In the *Certificate* dialog box, click the **Details** tab.

Question 10	*What is the Certificate used for? Hint: Look at the Enhanced Key Usage field.*

33. Click **OK** to close the *Certificate* dialog box.

34. Click **OK** to close the *Encrypting File System* dialog box.

Question 11	*Looking at the User Access to test.txt dialog box, who has a Recovery Certificate?*

35. Click **OK** to close the *User Access to Test* dialog box.

36. Click **OK** to close the *Advanced Attributes* dialog box.

37. Click **OK** to close the Test *Properties* dialog boxes.

38. On *Win8B*, log out of the administrator account and log on using the **User2** account and the **Pa$$w0rd** password.

39. Click the **Desktop** tile, click **File Explorer**, open the **C:\Data** folder, and then open the **test.txt** file.

Question 12	*Where you able to open the file?*

40. On *Win8B*, sign out as **User2**.

End of exercise. Close all windows on RWDC01 and Win8A.

Exercise 8.3	Encrypting a Volume with BitLocker
Overview	In this exercise, you will create a new volume and then use BitLocker to encrypt the entire volume.
Mindset	EFS will only encrypt individual files and folders; BitLocker can encrypt an entire volume. In other words, to encrypt an entire drive on a laptop, you can use BitLocker.
Completion time	25 minutes

1. On *Win8B*, log on using the **contoso\administrator** account and the **Pa$$w0rd** password. Click the **Desktop** tile.

2. Click the **File Explorer** icon on the taskbar. Click the **This PC** node.

3. Verify that you have an E drive. If you do not have an E drive, follow these steps:

   1. Right-click **This PC** and choose **Manage**.

   2. On the *Computer Management* page, click **Disk Management**.

   3. In the *Initialize Disk* dialog box, click **OK**.

   4. Right-click the **Unallocated** space for *Disk 1* and choose **New Simple Volume**.

   5. On the *New Simple Volume Wizard* page, click **Next**.

   6. On the *Specify Volume Size* page, click **Next**.

   7. On the *Assign Drive Letter or Path* page, click **Next**.

   8. On the *Format Partition* page, click **Next**.

   9. On the *Completing the New Simple Volume Wizard* page, click **Finish**.

   10. Close **Computer Management**.

   11. Close any dialog boxes that prompt you to format a disk by clicking Cancel.

4. Close **File Explorer**.

5. Right-click the **Start** menu and choose **Control Panel**.

6. Click **System and Security > BitLocker Drive Encryption**. The *BitLocker Drive Encryption* window opens (see Figure 8-3).

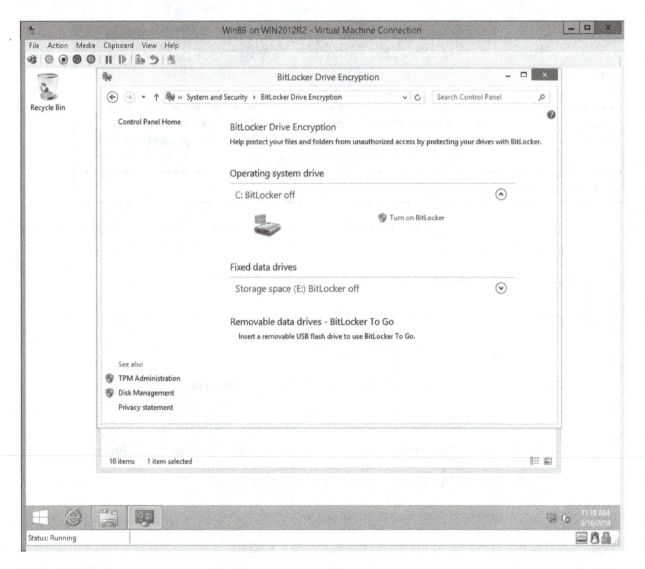

Figure 8-3
The *BitLocker Drive Encryption* window

7. Click the down arrow next to the *Storage space (E:)* drive and then click **Turn on BitLocker**. A *BitLocker Drive Encryption (E:)* window opens.

Question 13	Which two methods can be used to unlock a drive?

8. On the *Choose how you want to unlock this drive* page, click to select **Use a password to unlock the drive**. In the *Enter your password* text box and in the *Reenter your password* text box, type **Pa$$w0rd** and then click **Next**.

9. On the *How do you want to back up your recovery key?* page, click **Save to a file**.

10. In the *Save BitLocker recovery key as* dialog box, type **\\rwdc01\Software** before *BitLocker Recovery Key <GUID>.txt* and then click **Save**. Click **Next**.

11. On the *Are you ready to encrypt this drive?* page, click **Start encrypting**.

12. Take a screen shot of the *BitLocker Drive Encryption* window by pressing **Alt+PrtScr** and then paste it into your Lab 8 worksheet file in the page provided by pressing **Ctrl+V**.

13. When the drive is encrypted, close the *BitLocker Drive Encryption* window.

End of exercise. Close all windows on Win8B.

Exercise 8.4	Using Dynamic Access Control (DAC)
Overview	In this exercise, you will configure Dynamic Access Control by enabling KDC support for claims and creating a resource property and resource rule.
Mindset	Dynamic Access Control (DAC), originally called claims-based access control, was introduced with Windows Sever 2012, which is used for access management. It provides an automatic mechanism to secure and control access to resources.
Completion time	40 minutes

1. On *RWDC01*, log on using the **contoso\administrator** account and the **Pa$$w0rd** password.

2. In *Server Manager*, click **Tools > Group Policy Management**.

3. In the *Group Policy Management* console, expand **contoso.com**, and then expand **Domain Controllers**. Right-click **Default Domain Controllers Policy** and choose **Edit**.

4. In the *Group Policy Management Editor* window, navigate to **Computer Configuration\Policies\Administrative Templates\System\KDC** and double-click **KDC support for claims, compound authentication, and Kerberos Armoring**.

5. Click **Enabled**. Under *Options*, **Supported** is already selected.

6. Take a screen shot of the *KDC support for claims, compound authentication and Kerberos Armoring* dialog box by pressing **Alt+PrtScr** and then paste it into your Lab 8 worksheet file in the page provided by pressing **Ctrl+V**.

7. Click **OK** to close the *KDC support for claims, compound authentication, and Kerberos armoring* dialog box.

8. Close **Group Policy Management Editor**.

9. Close **Group Policy Management**.

10. On *RWDC01*, using **Server Manager**, click **Tools > Active Directory Administrative Center**. The *Active Directory Administrative Center* opens.

11. Navigate to the **Dynamic Access Control** node and click the **Claim Types** container, as shown in Figure 8-4.

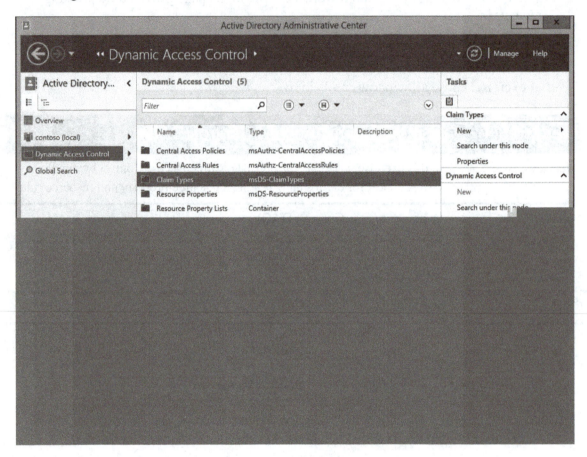

Figure 8-4
Opening Dynamic Access Control

12. In the *Tasks* pane, under *Claim Types*, click **New**, and then click **Claim Type**. The *Create Claim Type* dialog box opens.

13. With *User* already selected on the right side of the dialog box, under *Source Attribute*, scroll down and click **department**.

Question 14	What is the default display name?

14. Click **OK** to close the *Create Claim Type* dialog box.

15. In the *Tasks* pane, under *Claim Types*, click **New**, and then click **Claim Type**.

16. Under *Source Attribute*, scroll down and click **description**.

17. Click to deselect **User** and click to select **Computer**.

18. Click **OK** to close the *Create Claim Type* dialog box.

19. In *Active Directory Administrative Center*, click the **Dynamic Access Control** node and then double-click **Resource Properties**.

20. To enable the *Department* resource property, under *Resource Properties*, right-click **Department** and choose **Enable**.

21. To enable the *Confidentiality* resource property, under Resource Properties, right-click **Confidentiality** and choose **Enable**. Close Resource Properties.

22. Close **Active Directory Administrative Center**.

23. Log into Server02 as **contoso\administrator** with the password of **Pa$$w0rd**.

24. Open the **File Explorer** icon on the **Taskbar**.

25. Create the **C:\SharedFolder**.

26. Open the **C:\SharedFolder**. Right-click the empty white space of the **SharedFolder** window and choose **New > Rich Text Document**.

27. For the name of the document, type **Doc1** and then press **Enter**.

28. On *Server02*, using **Server Manager**, click **Tools > File Server Resource Manager**. If the File *Server Resource Manager* is not present, install the *File Server Resource Manager* by clicking **Manage > Add Roles and Features**. When you get to select server roles, *File Server Resource Manager* is located at **File and Storage Services > File and iSCSI Services > File Server Resource Manager**.

29. When *File Server Resource Manager* opens, expand **Classification Management** and then click **Classification Properties**.

30. Right-click **Classification Properties** and choose **Refresh**.

> | **Question 15** | *What are the two classifications properties that have a global scope?* |

31. Click **Classification Rules**.

32. Right-click **Classification Rules** and choose **Create Classification Rule**. The *Create Classification Rule* dialog box opens.

33. In the *General* tab, in the *Rule name* text box, type **Confidentiality**.

34. Click the **Scope** tab.

35. At the bottom of the dialog box, click **Add**. Browse to the **C:\SharedFolder** folder and then click **OK**.

36. Click the **Classification** tab.

37. The *Classification* method should already be *Content Classifier* and the property to be assigned to files and its value are, respectively, *Confidentiality* and *High*. To configure the *Classification* parameter, under *Parameters*, click **Configure**. The *Classification Parameters* dialog box opens.

38. Change the *Regular expression* to **String**. Under *Expression*, type **HR**, as shown in Figure 8-5. This means that if any document includes the string **HR**, it will be automatically be tagged as High confidentiality.

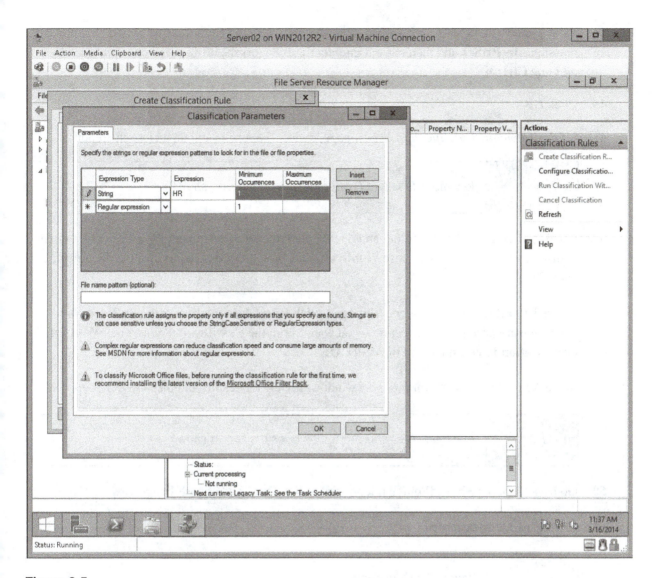

Figure 8-5
Defining a classification parameter

39. Click **OK** to close the *Classification Parameters* dialog box.

40. Click **Evaluation Type** tab.

41. **Click** to select **Re-evaluate existing property values**. Then select **Overwrite the existing value**.

42. Click **OK** to close the *Create Classification Rule* dialog box.

43. In *File Server Resource Manager*, under the *Actions* pane, click **Run Classification with All Rules Now**. When you are prompted to confirm that you want to run the classification rules, click **Wait for classification to complete**.

44. Take a screen shot of *File Server Resource Manager* with the *Run Classification* dialog box by pressing **Alt+PrtScr** and then paste it into your Lab 8 worksheet file in the page provided by pressing **Ctrl+V**.

45. Click **OK**.

46. On the *Automatic Classification Report* page, review the results and then close the report.

Question 16	How many files and properties does the report show?

47. Go to the **C:\SharedFolder** folder and double-click the **Doc1** document. When the Doc1 opens with WordPad, type **HR** and close WordPad. When you are prompted to save the document, click **Save**.

48. Go back to **File Server Resource Manager**, click **Run Classification with All Rules Now**. When you are prompted to select how you want to run the classification rules, click **Wait for classification to complete** and then click **OK**.

49. In the *Automatic Classification Report* window, review the results and then close the report.

Question 17	How many files and properties does the report show?

50. Go back to the **C:\SharedFolder** folder. Right-click **Doc1** and choose **Properties**.

51. Click the **Classification** tab.

Question 18	What is the Confidentiality set to?

52. Take a screen shot of the *Doc1 Properties* dialog box by pressing **Alt+PrtScr** and then paste it into your Lab 8 worksheet file in the page provided by pressing **Ctrl+V**.

53. Click **OK** to close the *Properties* dialog box.

54. Close **File Server Resource Manager**. Close all other open windows.

End of exercise. Close any open windows before you begin the next exercise.

Lab Challenge	Using BitLocker To Go
Overview	Since BitLocker To Go is used with removable disks, in this lab challenge, you will demonstrate using BitLocker to Go by writing the high-level steps for the following scenario. This is a written exercise.
Mindset	When BitLocker was released, it supported only local fixed disks. To support removable USB disks, Microsoft released BitLocker To Go. In this Lab Challenge, you are an administrator for the Contoso Corporation and you want to protect files stored on USB removable drives. You decide to encrypt the content of these drives using BitLocker To Go.
Completion time	5 minutes

Write out the general steps you performed to complete the challenge.

End of lab.

LAB 9
MANAGING HARDWARE AND PRINTERS

BEFORE YOU BEGIN

The lab environment consists of student workstations connected to a local area network, along with a server that functions as the domain controller for a domain called contoso.com. The computers required for this lab are listed in Table 9-1.

Table 9-1
Computers Required for Lab 9

Computer	Operating System	Computer Name
Server	Windows Server 2012 R2	RWDC01
Server	Windows Server 2012 R2	Server02
Client	Windows 8.1.1	Win8A

In addition to the computers, you will also need the software listed in Table 9-2 to complete Lab 9.

Table 9-2
Software Required for Lab 9

Software	Location
Lab 9 student worksheet	Lab09_worksheet.docx (provided by instructor)

Working with Lab Worksheets

Each lab in this manual requires that you answer questions, shoot screen shots, and perform other activities that you will document in a worksheet named for the lab, such as Lab09_worksheet.docx. You will find these worksheets on the book companion site. It is recommended that you use a USB flash drive to store your worksheets so you can submit them to your instructor for review. As you perform the exercises in each lab, open the appropriate worksheet file, fill in the required information, and then save the file to your flash drive.

SCENARIO

After completing this lab, you will be able to:

- Install drivers with Device Manager

- Roll back drivers

- Use Device Manager to identify problems with drivers

- Install a printer on a print server

- Use Reliability Monitor to identify potential problems

- Use Task Manager to manage processes and analyze performance

- Use Resource Monitor and Performance Monitor to identify performance problems.

- Create a group policy to enable driver signing

Estimated lab time: 145 minutes

Exercise 9.1	Working with Device Manager
Overview	In this exercise, you will update device drivers with Device Manager.
Mindset	Device Manager gives you a graphical tool to manage devices and device drivers.
Completion time	30 minutes

1. On *Win8A*, log on using the **contoso\administrator** account and the **Pa$$w0rd** password. Click the **Desktop** tile.

2. Right-click the **Start button** and choose **Device Manager**.

Question 1	Are there any errors or unknown devices?

3. Expand the **Ports (COM & LPT)** node (see Figure 9-1).

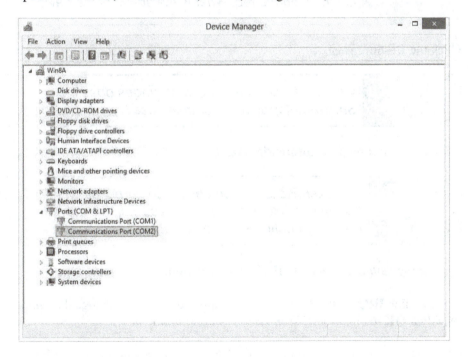

Figure 9-1
Expanding the Ports (COM & LPT) node

4. Right-click **Communications Port (COM2)** and choose **Disable**.

5. When you are prompted to confirm that you really want to disable the device, click **Yes**.

Question 2	Which icon represents a disabled device?

6. Right-click **Communications Port (COM2)** and choose **Enable**.

7. Right-click **Communications Port (COM2)** and choose **Properties**.

Question 3	On the General tab, what is the status of the device?

8. Click the **Resources** tab.

Question 4	What IRQ and I/O port range is Com2 using?

9. Click **OK** to close the *Communications Port (COM2) Properties* dialog box.

10. Expand the **Floppy drive controllers** node.

11. Right-click **Standard floppy disk controller** and choose **Properties**.

Question 5	On the General tab, what is the status of the device?

12. Click the **Resources** tab.

Question 6	Which IRQ, DMA and I/O port ranges does the Standard floppy disk controller use?

13. Click to deselect the **Use automatic settings**.

Note	This exercise is for demonstration purposes only. Today, it would be extremely rare that you will ever have to manually configure these settings.

14. Change the *Setting based on* to **Basic configuration 0002**.

15. Double-click **IRQ**. In the *Edit Interrupt Request* dialog box, change the *Value* to **05**. Click **OK** to close the *Edit Interrupt Request* dialog box.

16. Click **OK** to close the *Standard floppy disk controller Properties* dialog box.

17. When you are prompted to confirm that you want to continue, click **Yes**.

18. When you are prompted to restart the computer, click **No**.

Question 7	Which icon does the Standard floppy disk controller have now?

19. Double-click **Standard floppy disk controller**.

Question 8	What is the device status now?

20. Click the **Resources** tab.

21. Click **Set Configuration Manually**.

22. Click to select **Use automatic settings**.

23. Click **OK** to close the *Standard floppy disk controller Properties* dialog box.

24. When you are prompted to restart the computer, click **Yes**.

25. On *Win8A*, log on using the **contoso\administrator** account and the **Pa$$w0rd** password. Click the **Desktop** tile.

26. Right-click the **Start** button and choose **Device Manager**.

27. Right-click **Win8A** and choose **Scan for hardware changes**.

28. Expand the **Ports (COM and LPT)** node and then click **Communications Port (COM2) port**.

29. Right-click **Communications Port (COM2) port** and choose **Update Driver Software**.

30. On the *How do you want to search for driver software?* page, click **Search automatically for updated driver software**.

Question 9	Which driver was located and what information was provided about the driver?

31. Click **Close** to close the *Update Driver Software – Communications Port (COM2)* dialog box.

32. Right-click **Communications port (COM2)** and choose **Properties**.

33. Click the **Driver** tab.

Question 10	Which driver version is being used by Communication Port (COM2)?

34. Click **Update Driver**.

35. On the *How do you want to search for driver software?* page, click **Browse my computer for driver software**.

36. On the *Browse for driver software on your computer* page, click **Let me pick from a list of device drivers on my computer**.

37. On the *Select the device driver you want to install for this hardware* page, click to deselect the **Show compatible hardware**.

Note	This is for demonstration purposes only. Normally, you want to use drivers that are compatible.

38. For the *Manufacturer*, click **Trimble** and then click **Trimble PCMCIA GPS Adapter (Rev. B)**. Click **Next**.

39. When an update driver warning is displayed, click **Yes**.

40. When the driver has been installed, click **Close**.

41. Take a screen shot of the *Trimble PCMCIA GPS Adapter (Rev. B) (COM2) Properties* dialog box by pressing **Alt+PrtScr** and then paste it into your Lab 9 worksheet file in the page provided by pressing **Ctrl+V**.

42. Click **Close** to close the *Trimble PCMCIA GPS Adapter (Rev. B) (COM2) Properties* dialog box.

End of exercise. Leave Device Manager open for the next exercise.

Exercise 9.2	Rolling Back a Device Driver
Overview	In this exercise, you will use Device Manager to rollback a device driver.
Mindset	Sometimes when you upgrade or load a device driver, the device that the device driver is used for stops working or causes other problems with Windows. With Device Manager, you can roll back a device driver to the previous device driver.
Completion time	5 minutes

1. On *Win8A*, using *Device Manager*, right-click **Trimble PCMCIA GPS Adapter (Rev. B) (COM2)** and choose **Properties**. The *Trimble PCMCIA GPS Adapter (Rev. B) (COM2) Properties* dialog box opens.

2. Click the **Driver** tab.

3. Click **Roll Back Driver**.

Question 11	Which option would you have clicked to manually pick a driver to install?

4. When you are prompted to confirm that you are sure you would like to roll back to the previously installed driver software, click **Yes**.

5. Take a screen shot of the *Communications Port (COM2) Properties* dialog box by pressing **Alt+PrtScr** and then paste it into your Lab 9 worksheet file in the page provided by pressing **Ctrl+V**.

6. Click **Close** to close the *Communications Port (COM2) Properties* dialog box.

End of exercise. Close the Device Manager on Win8A but leave Win8A logged on for the next exercise.

Exercise 9.3	Managing Print Servers and Printers
Overview	In this exercise, you will first create a new server and then you will install and configure Windows Deployment Services so that you can quickly install Windows servers in the future.
Mindset	Sharing printers was one of the earliest network services and remains an essential service needed by just about every organization. To centralize the management of printers, Windows Server 2012 R2 features Print and Document Services, which includes the Print Management console.
Completion time	30 minutes

First, you will install the print and document services by performing the following steps:

1. On *Server02*, using *Server Manager*, click **Manage > Add Roles and Features**.

2. On the *Add Roles and Features Wizard* page, click **Next**.

3. On the *Select installation type* page, click **Next**.

4. On the *Select destination server* page, click **Next**.

5. On the *Select server roles* page, select **Print and Document Services**. When you are prompted to add features, click **Add Features**.

6. Back on the *Select server roles* page, click **Next**.

7. On the *Select features* page, click **Next**.

8. On the *Print and Document Services* page, click **Next**.

9. On the *Select role services* page, *Print Server* is already selected. Click **Next**.

10. On the *Confirm installation selections* page, click **Install**.

11. When the installation is completed, take a screen shot of the *Installation progress* page by pressing **Alt+PrtScr** and then paste it into your Lab 9 worksheet file in the page provided by pressing **Ctrl+V**.

12. Click **Close**.

Next, you will install a local printer by performing the following steps:

1. Using *Server Manager*, click **Tools > Print Management**. The *Print Management* console opens (see Figure 9-2).

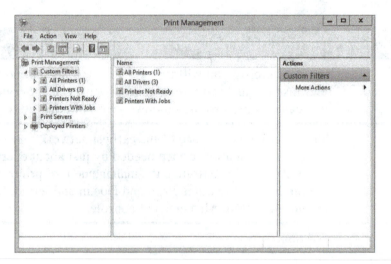

Figure 9-2
The Print Management console

2. Expand the **Print Servers** node and then click **Server02 (local)**.

3. Right-click **Server02 (local)** and choose **Add Printer**.

4. On the *Printer Installation* page, click to select **Add a new printer using an existing port**. *LPT1: (Printer Port)* is already selected. Click **Next**.

5. On the *Printer Driver* page, *Install a new driver* is already selected. Click **Next**.

6. On the *Printer Installation* page, for the *Manufacturer* setting, click **HP**. For the *Printer* setting, click **HP Color LaserJet 2500 PCL6 Class Driver** and then click **Next**.

7. On the *Printer Name and Sharing Settings* page, answer the following question and then click **Next**.

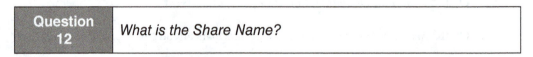

Question 12	What is the Share Name?

8. On the *Printer Found* page, click **Next**.

9. When the printer is installed, click **Finished**.

10. Using *Print Management*, under *Server02 (local)*, click the **Printers** node.

11. Take a screen shot of the *Print Management* window by pressing **Alt+PrtScr** and then paste it into your Lab 9 worksheet file in the page provided by pressing **Ctrl+V**.

12. Right-click the **HP Color LaserJet 2500 PCL 6 Class Driver** printer and choose **Properties**.

13. Click the **Sharing** tab. Notice the *Share* name.

14. For the printer to be listed in Active Directory, click to select **List in the directory**.

15. Click the **Ports** tab. Notice the port that is assigned.

16. Click the **Security** tab.

Question 13	Who is allowed to print to this printer?

17. Click the **Administrators** group.

Question 14	Which permissions are assigned to administrator?

18. Click **Everyone** again.

19. Select the **Allow Manage documents** permission.

20. Click **OK** to close the *HP Color LaserJet 2500 PCL Class Driver Properties* dialog box.

Next, you will install a network printer by performing the following steps:

1. Under *Server02 (local)*, right-click the **Printers** node and choose **Add Printer**.

2. On the *Printer Installation* page, click **Create a new port and add a new printer** and then click **Next**.

3. In the *Port Name* dialog box, in the *Enter a port name* text box, type **Printer1**. Click **OK**.

4. Back in the *Printer Driver* dialog box, *Install a new driver* is already selected. Click **Next**.

5. For the *Manufacturer* setting, click **HP**. For the *Printers* setting, click **HP Color LaserJet 2700 PS Class Driver** and then click **Next**.

6. In the *Printer Name and Sharing Settings* dialog box, answer the following question and then click **Next**.

Question 15	What is the Share Name?

7. On the *Printer Found* page, click **Next**.

8. When the wizard is complete, click **Finish**.

9. Take a screen shot of the *Print Management* window by pressing **Alt+PrtScr** and then paste it into your Lab 9 worksheet file in the page provided by pressing **Ctrl+V**.

10. Right-click **HP Color LaserJet 2700 PS Class Driver** and choose **Properties**.

11. In the *HP Color LaserJet 2700 PS Class Driver Properties* dialog box, click the **Sharing** tab.

12. Click to select the **List in the directory**.

13. Click **OK** to close the *HP Color LaserJet 2700 PS Class Driver Properties* dialog box.

14. Close the **Print Management** console.

Lastly, you will install printers on Windows 8.1 by performing the following steps:

1. On *Win8A*, on the taskbar, click the **File Explorer** icon to open *File Explorer*.

2. Using *File Explorer*, navigate to **\\server02**.

3. Right-click **HP Color LaserJet 2500 PCL6 Class Driver** and choose **Connect**.

4. Open the **Charms** bar by moving the mouse pointer to the top-right corner, clicking **Settings**, and then clicking **Change PC Settings**.

5. Under *PC settings*, click **PC and devices**, and then click **Devices**.

6. Take a screen shot of the *PC settings* screen showing the new printer by pressing **Alt+PrtScr** and then paste it into your Lab 9 worksheet file in the page provided by pressing **Ctrl+V**.

7. Click **Add a device**.

8. Click **HP Color Laserjet 2700 PS Class Driver**.

9. Take a screen shot of the *PC settings* page showing the second printer by pressing **Alt+PrtScr** and then paste it into your Lab 9 worksheet file in the page provided by pressing **Ctrl+V**.

10. Press **Alt+F4**.

End of exercise. Log off of Server02.

Exercise 9.4	Using the Reliability Monitor
Overview	Reliability Monitor is a somewhat obscure tool that can determine the reliability of a system, including allowing you to see whether any recent changes have been made to the system itself. In this exercise, you will open Reliability Monitor to check the status of the computer.
Mindset	Reliability Monitor is a Control Panel/Action Panel tool that measures hardware and software problems and other changes to your computer that could affect the reliability of the computer.
Completion time	10 minutes

1. On *Win8A*, click **Start**, type **regedit**, and then press **Enter**. The *Registry Editor* opens.

2. In the left pane, navigate to the *HKEY_LOCAL_MACHINE\SOFTWARE\Microsoft\Reliability Analysis\WMI* node.

3. In the right pane, double-click **WMIEnable**. In the *Value data* text box, ensure that the value data is set to **1**, as shown in Figure 9-3. Click **OK**.

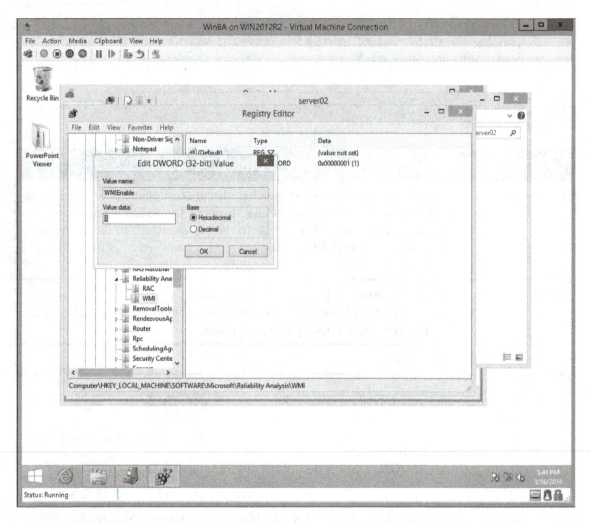

Figure 9-3
Changing the WMIEnable value

4. Close the **Registry Editor**.

5. Right-click the **Start** button and choose **Computer Management**. *Computer Management* opens.

6. In the left pane, navigate to the **Computer Management > Task Scheduler > Task Scheduler Library > Microsoft > Windows > RAC**.

7. Ensure that the **RacTask** is set to *Enable* and that it is running.

8. Close **Task Scheduler**.

9. Open the **Start** menu, type **perfmon /rel**, and then press **Enter**. The *Reliability Monitor* opens.

10. Take a screen shot of the *Reliability Monitor* page by pressing **Alt+PrtScr** and then paste it into your Lab 9 worksheet file in the page provided by pressing **Ctrl+V**.

11. At the bottom of the screen, click **View all problem reports**.

Question 16	*Were there any problems reported?*

12. Click **OK** to close the *Problem Reports* window.

13. Close *Reliability Monitor* by clicking **OK**.

End of exercise. On Win8A, close the *Computer Management* console.

Exercise 9.5	Using Task Manager
Overview	In this exercise, you will use Task Manager to look at the primary performance systems. In addition, you will view and manage running processes.
Mindset	Task Manager is one of the handiest programs you can use to take a quick glance at performance to see which programs are using the most system resources on your computer. You can see the status of running programs and programs that have stopped responding, and you can stop a program running in memory.
Completion time	20 minutes

1. On *Win8A*, right-click the **Taskbar** and choose **Task Manager**.

Question 17	*What applications are running?*

Question 18	*What tabs are shown?*

2. Click **More Details**.

Question 19	*What tabs are shown?*

3. Open **WordPad**.

Question 20	*In the Apps section, what processes are used for WordPad?*

4. On Task Manager, click **Fewer details**.

5. Right-click **Windows Wordpad Application** and choose **End Task**.

6. Start **WordPad** again.

7. On *Task Manager*, click **More details**.

8. Right-click **Windows Wordpad Application** and choose **Open file location**. The *Accessories* folder opens.

9. Close the **Accessories** folder.

Question 21	How much memory is WordPad using?

10. Right-click the **Name** title at the top of the first column and choose **Process name** (as shown in Figure 9-4).

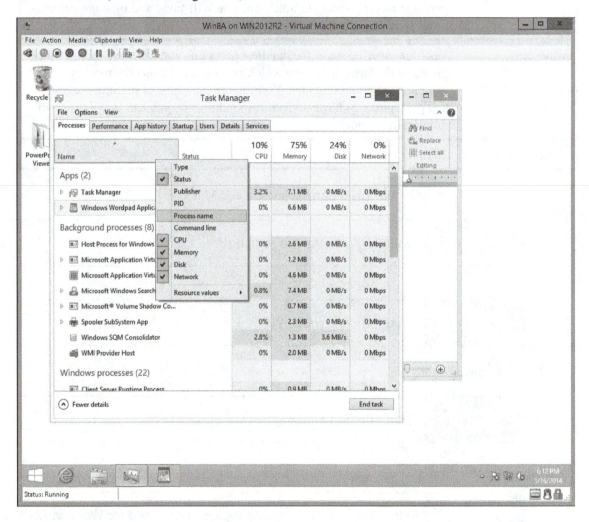

Figure 9-4
Adding the Process name so that it can also be displayed

11. Right-click **Windows WordPad Application** and choose **End Task**.

12. Click the **Performance** tab.

Question 22	What are the primary systems that you can monitor with Task Manager?

Question 23	How many virtual processors is Win8A using?

13. Click **Memory** and **Ethernet** to view what each option has to offer.

14. Click the **Users** tab.

15. Expand **Administrator** to display the programs and processes being executed by the administrator.

16. To see a detailed list of all processes running, click the **Details** tab.

17. To display additional columns, right-click the **Name** column title and choose **Select columns**.

18. In the *Select columns* dialog box, click to select **Session ID** and **Threads**. Click **OK**.

19. Take a screen shot of the *Task Manager* window by pressing **Alt+PrtScr** and then paste it into your Lab 9 worksheet file in the page provided by pressing **Ctrl+V**.

20. To sort by components that make up the most memory, click the **Memory (private work set)** title.

21. Occasionally a program or action might cause Windows Explorer to stop functioning. In these cases, you can use Task Manager to stop and restart Explorer. Therefore, find and right-click **explorer.exe** and choose **End task**.

22. When you are prompted to confirm that you want to end explorer.exe, click **End process**.

23. Click **File > Run new task**.

24. In the *Create new task* dialog box, in the *Open* text box, type **explorer** and then click **OK**.

25. To view the current services, click the **Services** tab.

26. Close **Task Manager**.

End of exercise. Close all windows on Win8A.

Exercise 9.6	Using Resource Monitor
Overview	In this exercise, you will use Resource Manager to monitor server resources.
Mindset	Resource Monitor is a system tool that allows you to view information about the use of hardware (CPU, memory, disk, and network) and software resources (file handlers and modules) in real time.
Completion time	10 minutes

1. On *Win8A*, click **Start**, type **perfmon**, and then press **Enter**. *Performance Monitor* opens. In the *Overview* section, click the **Open Resource Monitor** link. (Minimize the *Performance Monitor* window for the next exercise).

Question 24	What are the primary systems that you can monitor with Resource Monitor?

2. Click the **CPU** tab.

3. To sort the processes alphabetically, click the **Image** title at the top of the first column in the *Processes* section.

4. Take a screen shot of the *Resource Monitor* window by pressing **Alt+PrtScr** and then paste it into your Lab 9 worksheet file in the page provided by pressing **Ctrl+V**.

5. Click the **Memory** tab and then click the **Working Set (KB)** column to sort memory usage.

Question 25	What process is using the most memory?

6. Click the **Disk** tab.

Question 26	What process is using the disk the most?

7. Click the **Network** tab and expand **TCP Connections**.

Question 27	What local ports are being used by spoolsv.exe?

8. Close the **Resource Monitor**.

End of exercise. Close all windows on Win8A.

Exercise 9.7	Using Performance Monitor
Overview	Although Task Manager and Resource Manager provide you with a quick look at your system performance, Performance Monitor allows you to thoroughly exam the performance of a system. In this exercise, you will open Performance Monitor and show various counters over a period of time.
Mindset	Performance Monitor is an MMC snap-in that provides tools for analyzing system performance. From a single console, you can monitor application and hardware performance in real time, specify which data you want to collect in logs, define thresholds for alerts and automatic actions, generate reports, and view past performance data in a variety of ways.
Completion time	30 minutes

First, you will learn to use counters with Performance Monitor:

1. On *Win8A*, maximize *Performance Monitor* from the previous exercise.

2. Browse to and click **Monitoring Tools\Performance Monitor**.

3. Click **% Processor Time** at the bottom of the screen. To remove the counter, click the **Delete (red X)** button at the top of the Window.

4. Click the **Add** (green plus (+) sign) button in the toolbar. The *Add Counters* dialog box appears.

5. Under *Available counters*, expand **Processor**, click **% Processor Time**, and then click **Show description**, as shown in Figure 9-5. Read the description for *% Processor Time*.

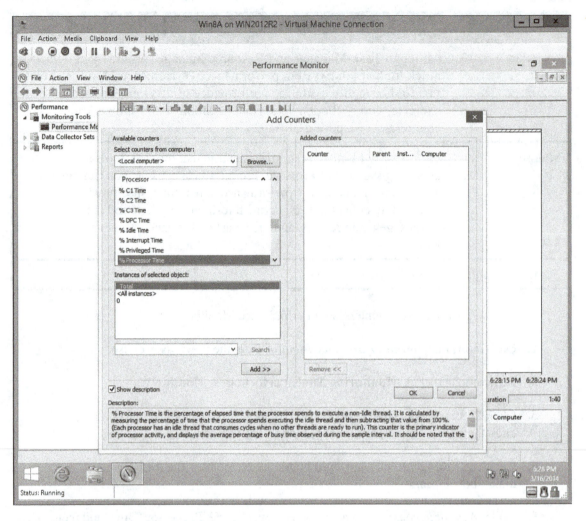

Figure 9-5
Looking at a description of a counter

6. Click **Add**. *% Processor Time* should show up in the *Added counters* section.

7. Under *Available counters*, expand the **Server Work Queues** and click the **Queue Length** counter. Under Instances of selected objects, click **0**. Then click **Add**.

8. Add the following counters:

   ● *System:* **Processor Queue Length**

   ● *Memory:* **Page Faults/Sec**

   ● *Memory:* **Pages/Sec**

   ● *PhysicalDisk (_Total):* **Current Disk Queue Length**

9. Click **OK** to close the *Add Counters* dialog box.

10. Open **Task Manager** and then close **Task Manager**. You should see a spike in CPU usage.

11. At the top of the graph, you will see a toolbar with 13 buttons. Click the down arrow of the **Change graph type** (the third button) and then click **Histogram bar**.

12. Change the graph type to **Report**.

13. Change back to the **Line graph**.

14. Click the **Properties** button (the fifth button from the end) on the toolbar. The *Performance Monitor Properties* sheet appears. Notice the counters that you have selected.

15. Click **Processor (_Total)\\%Processor Time**.

16. Change the width to heaviest line width. Change the color to **Red**.

17. Click the **Graph** tab.

18. In the *Vertical scale* box, change the value of the *Maximum* field to **200** and then click **OK**.

Next, you will learn to use Data Collector Sets (DCS):

1. In the left pane, expand **Data Collector Sets**.

2. Right-click the **User Defined** folder and choose **New > Data Collector Set**. In the *Name:* text box, type **MyDCS1**.

3. Click **Create manually (Advanced)** and then click **Next**.

4. When you are prompted to select the type of data do you want to include, click **Performance Counter** and then click **Next**.

5. To add counters, click **Add**.

6. Under *Available Counters*, expand the **Processor** node by clicking the down arrow next to *Processor*. Scroll down and click **%Processor Time**. Click **Add**.

7. Add the following counters.

   ● *Server Work Queues:* **Queue Length**
   ● *System:* **Processor Queue Length**
   ● *Memory:* **Page Faults/Sec**
   ● *Memory:* **Pages/Sec**
   ● *PhysicalDisk (_Total):* **Current Disk Queue Length**

8. Click **OK** and click then click **Next**.

9. Click **Finish**.

10. Right-click **MyDCS1** and choose **Start**.

11. Let it run for at least two minutes.

12. Right-click **MyDCS1** and choose **Stop**.

13. Open **File Explorer** and navigate to **c:\PerfLogs\Admin\MyDCS1**. Then open the folder that was just created.

14. Double-click **DataCollector01.blg**. The *Performance Monitor* graph opens.

Question 28	*Now that the DCS has been created, what advantages does the MyDCS1 present?*

15. Take a screen shot of the *Performance Monitor* graph by pressing **Alt+PrtScr** and then paste it into your Lab 9 worksheet file in the page provided by pressing **Ctrl+V**.

16. Close the *Performance Monitor* graph and then close the *MyDCS1* folder.

17. Close **Performance Monitor**.

End of exercise. Close all windows on Win8A.

Lab Challenge	Creating a Group Policy to Enable Driver Signing
Overview	To complete this challenge, you will create a group policy to ensure that the driver signing is enabled.
Mindset	Driver signing is used to ensure the device drivers used by Windows include a digital signature that indicates who the publisher is and if the driver has been altered. It is highly recommended that you use only Driver signing.
Completion time	10 minutes

Write out the steps you performed to complete the challenge.

End of lab.

LAB 10
MANAGING MOBILE DEVICES

THIS LAB CONTAINS THE FOLLOWING EXERCISES AND ACTIVITIES:

Exercise 10.1   Installing the Microsoft Diagnostic and Recovery Toolkit 8.1

Exercise 10.2   Creating Microsoft Diagnostic and Recovery Toolkit 8.1 Boot Images

Exercise 10.3   Using Windows Performance Toolkit

Exercise 10.4   Creating a Mobile Device Mailbox Policy

Exercise 10.5   Configuring SSL on the Exchange ActiveSync Virtual Directory

Exercise 10.6   Syncing your Computer

Exercise 10.7   Using a Work Folder

Lab Challenge   Performing a Mobile Device Remote Wipe

BEFORE YOU BEGIN

The lab environment consists of student workstations connected to a local area network, along with a server that functions as the domain controller for a domain called contoso.com. The computers required for this lab are listed in Table 10-1.

Table 10-1
Computers Required for Lab 10

Computer	Operating System	Computer Name
Server	Windows Server 2012 R2	RWDC01
Server	Windows Server 2012 R2	Server01
Server	Windows Server 2012 R2	Server03
Workstation	Windows 8.1	Win8A

In addition to the computers, you will also need the software listed in Table 10-2 to complete Lab 10.

Table 10-2
Software Required for Lab 10

Software	Location
Lab 10 student worksheet	Lab10_worksheet.docx (provided by instructor)

Working with Lab Worksheets

Each lab in this manual requires that you answer questions, shoot screen shots, and perform other activities that you will document in a worksheet named for the lab, such as Lab10_worksheet.docx. You will find these worksheets on the book companion site. It is recommended that you use a USB flash drive to store your worksheets so you can submit them to your instructor for review. As you perform the exercises in each lab, open the appropriate worksheet file, fill in the required information, and then save the file to your flash drive.

SCENARIO

After completing this lab, you will be able to:

- Install the Microsoft Diagnostic and Recovery Toolkit 8.1

- Create Microsoft Diagnostic and Recovery Toolkit 8 Boot Images

- Use Windows Performance Toolkit

- Create a mobile device mailbox policy

- Configure SSL on the Exchange ActiveSync Virtual Directory

- Sync your computer

- Use a Work Folder

- Perform a mobile device remote wipe

Estimated lab time: 140 minutes

Exercise 10.1	Installing the Microsoft Diagnostic and Recovery Toolkit 8.1
Overview	In this exercise, you will install the Microsoft Diagnostic and Recovery Toolkit from the Microsoft Desktop Optimization Pack.
Mindset	The Microsoft Diagnostic and Recovery Toolkit is a core component of the Microsoft Desktop Optimization Pack that allow administrators to easily and quickly recover computers that have become unusable.
Completion time	25 minutes

1. On *Win8A*, log on using the **contoso\administrator** account and the **Pa$$w0rd** password.

2. Click the **Desktop** tile.

3. On the taskbar, click the **File Explorer** icon to open *File Explorer*.

4. Open the **\\rwdc01\software\Windows Kits\8.1\ADK** folder.

5. In the *ADK* folder, double-click the **adksetup** application.

6. In the *Windows Assessment and Deployment Kit for Windows 8.1* page, on the *Specify Location* page, click **Next**.

7. On the *Join the Customer Experience Improvement Program (CEIP)* page, click **Next**.

8. On the *License Agreement* page, click **Accept**.

9. Click to deselect all options except *Deployment Tools, Windows Preinstallation Environment (Windows PE), and Windows Performance Toolkit* (see Figure 10-1). Click **Install**.

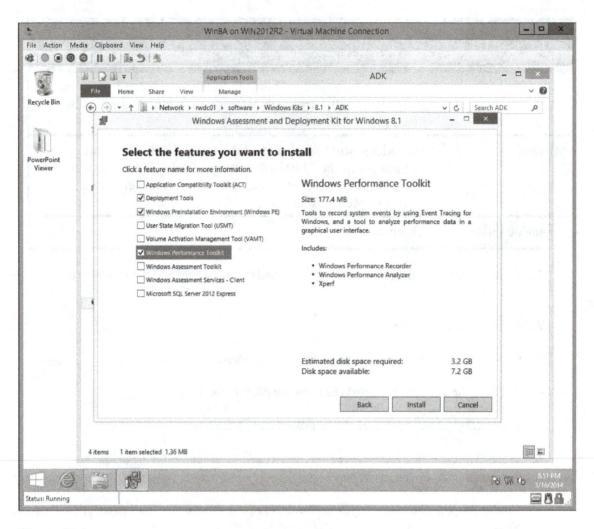

Figure 10-1
Installing the Assessment and Deployment Kit

10. Take a screen shot of the *Assessment and Deployment Kit for Windows 8.1* page by pressing **Alt+PrtScr** and then paste it into your Lab 10 worksheet file in the page provided by pressing **Ctrl+V**.

11. Click **Close**.

12. Using *File Explorer*, open **the \\rwdc01\software** folder. Right-click the **SW_DVD5_Dsktp_Optimization_Pck_SA_2013 R2_English_-2_MLF_X18-90519** ISO and choose **Mount**.

13. On the *MDOP drive* folder, double-click the **Launcher** folder and then double-click **launcher** HTML Application.

14. In the *Microsoft Desktop Optimization Pack for Software Assurance* screen (see Figure 10-2), click **Diagnostics and Recovery Toolset**.

Figure 10-2
The Microsoft Desktop Optimization Pack for Software Assurance screen

15. Under the *DaRT 8.1 for Windows 8.1 and Windows Server 2012R2* section, next to *DaRT 8.1*, click **64-bit**.

16. On the *Microsoft DaRT 8.1 Setup Wizard* screen, click **Next**.

17. On the *End-User License Agreement* screen, click **I Agree**.

18. Select **I don't want to use Microsoft Update** and then click **Next**.

19. On the *Select Installation Folder* screen, click **Next**.

20. On the *Setup Options* screen, answer the following question and then click **Next**.

Question 1	What are the three setup options?

21. Click **Install**.

22. When the *Completing the Microsoft DaRT 8.0 SP1 Setup Wizard* has been completed, take a screen shot of the *Microsoft DaRT 8.0 SP1 Setup Wizard* page by pressing **Alt+PrtScr** and then paste it into your Lab 10 worksheet file in the page provided by pressing **Ctrl+V**.

23. Click **Finish**.

End of exercise. Close the *Microsoft Diagnostics and Recovery Toolset* window, but leave the computer logged into for the next exercise.

Exercise 10.2	Creating Microsoft Diagnostic and Recovery Toolkit 8.1 Boot Images
Overview	In this exercise, you will use the Microsoft Diagnostic and Recovery Toolkit to create a DaRT recovery image that can be used to help fix computers running Windows 8.1 that will no longer boot.
Mindset	By using the DaRT Recovery Image Wizard, you can create the DaRT recovery image (ISO or WIM file) that can be burned to a bootable optical disk or which can be deployed from a remote network partition or on a recovery partition on a local disk.
Completion time	15 minutes

1. On *Win8A*, using *File Explorer*, open the **\\rwdc01\software** folder.

2. Right-click **9600.17050.WINBLUE_REFRESH.140317-1640_X64FRE_SERVER_EVAL_EN-US-IR3_SSSX64FREE_EN-US_DV9** and choose **Mount**.

Question 2	*Which driver letter is assigned to the Windows installation files?*

3. Click the **Start button** to open the *Start* screen. On the *Start* screen, click **All Programs** and then click the **DaRT Recovery Image** tile (the second tile under the *Microsoft DaRT 8.1* section).

4. On the *Microsoft DaRT Recovery Image Wizard* page, click **Next**.

5. On the *Windows 8.1 Media* screen, select **Create 64-bit DaRT image** and then specify **F:** as the root path to your Windows 8.1 installation media. Click **Next** to continue.

6. On the *Tools* screen, answer the following question and then click **Next** to install all of the tools available.

Question 3	*Which option would you use to set a password for a local account?*

7. On the *Remote Connection* screen, click **Next**.

8. On the *Advanced Options* page, click the **Crash Analyzer** tab. Make sure the option *Use the Debugging Tools from the computer that is being debugged* is selected.

9. Click the **Defender** tab and then click **Download the definitions later**. Click **Next**.

10. On the *Create Image* page, answer the following question and then click **Create**.

Question 4	Where will the created images be stored?

11. Once the *The DaRT image was successfully created* message appears, take a screen shot of the *Microsoft DaRT Recovery Image Wizard* dialog box by pressing **Alt+PrtScr** and then paste it into your Lab 10 worksheet file in the page provided by pressing **Ctrl+V**.

12. Click **Next**.

13. On the *Create Bootable Media* page, click **Close**.

14. Using *File Explorer*, right-click the **DVD Drive (E:)** and choose **Eject**.

End of exercise. Close any open windows before you begin the next exercise.

Exercise 10.3	Using Windows Performance Toolkit
Overview	In this exercise, you will run the Windows Performance Recorder to record performance to create an Event Tracing for Windows. You will then use the Windows Performance Analyzer to view the trace.
Mindset	The Windows Performance Toolkit contains the Windows Performance Recorder (WPR) and Windows Performance Analyzer (WPA). WPR is a recording tool that creates Event Tracing for Windows (ETW recordings), which can be analyzed when performing certain activities. WPA is a graphical analysis tool with graphic capabilities and data tables with full text search capabilities, which can help explore the root cause of performance problems.
Completion time	10 minutes

1. On *Win8A*, click the **Start** button to open the *Start* screen. On the *Start* screen, click **All Programs**, and then click the **Windows Performance Recorder** tile (the sixth tile under the *Windows Kits* section).

2. On the *Windows Performance Recorder* page, answer the following question and then click **Start**.

Question 5	What is the default Detail level? (You may need to click the More options arrow to see it).

3. Wait one minute. (Observe the *Time: timer* above the *Save* button). Then click **Save**.

4. In the description, type **Test** and then click **Save**.

5. When the *General* trace has been saved, click **Open in WPA**.

6. Click **System Activity**.

7. Double-click **System Activity**.

8. Double-click **Computation**.

9. Take a screen shot of the *Windows Performance Analyzer* by pressing **Alt+PrtScr** and then paste it into your Lab 10 worksheet file in the page provided by pressing **Ctrl+V**.

End of exercise. Close *Windows Performance Analyzer* and *Windows Performance Recorder*.

Exercise 10.4	Creating a Mobile Device Mailbox Policy
Overview	In this exercise, you will create a mobile device mailbox policy in Microsoft Exchange Server 2013.
Mindset	The mobile device mailbox policies settings are used to apply a common set of policies or security settings to a collection of users in Microsoft Exchange. After you deploy Exchange ActiveSync in your Exchange 2013 organization, you can create new mobile device mailbox policies or modify existing policies using the Exchange Control Panel.
Completion time	15 minutes

1. On *Win8A*, open **Internet Explorer** and then go to **https://server01/ecp**.

2. If a dialog box appears, warning you that you are about to view pages over a secure connection, click to select **In the future, do not show this warning** and then click **OK**.

3. If an *Internet Explorer* dialog box appears, warning you that content from the website listed below is being blocked by the Internet Explorer Enhanced Security Configuration, click **Add**. In the *Trusted sites* dialog box opens, click **Add** and then click **Close**.

4. When you are prompted for credentials for the Outlook Web App, log on using the **contoso\administrator** account and the **Pa$$w0rd** password.

5. On the *Exchange admin center* page (see Figure 10-3), in the left pane, click **mobile** and then, from the center pane, next to *mobile device access*, click **mobile device mailbox policies**.

Figure 10-3
The Exchange admin center page

6. In the center pane, click the **+** symbol to create a new mobile device mailbox policy.

7. In the *Name* field, type **My Mobile Policy**.

8. Click to select **This is the default policy**.

9. Click to select **Require a password**.

10. Click to select **Require an alphanumeric password**.

11. Under the *Password must include this many character sets* section, click the drop-down box and then select **3**.

12. Select **Minimum password length** and, in the field that appears, type **6**.

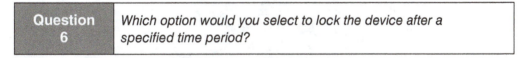

Question 6	Which option would you select to lock the device after a specified time period?

13. Select **Enforce password lifetime (days)** and, in the field that appears, type **60**.

14. Under *Password recycle count*, type **5**.

15. Click **Save**. The new policy appears in the middle pane.

16. Take a screen shot of the *mobile device mailbox policies* page by pressing **Alt+PrtScr** and then paste it into your Lab 10 worksheet file in the page provided by pressing **Ctrl+V**.

17. Close **Internet Explorer**.

End of exercise. Log off Win8A.

Exercise 10.5	Configuring SSL on the Exchange ActiveSync Virtual Directory
Overview	In this exercise, you will configure the Exchange ActiveSync virtual directory to use only SSL.
Mindset	Since ActiveSync traffic can contain confidential information, you must install digital certificates on the IIS website and you must configure the ActiveSync virtual directory to use only SSL (which will prevent HTTP traffic).
Completion time	10 minutes

1. On *Server01*, log on using the **contoso\administrator** account and the **Pa$$w0rd** password.

2. On *Server01*, using *Server Manager*, click **Tools > Internet Information Services (IIS) Manager**.

3. Click **SERVER01** (see Figure 10-4). If you are prompted to get the latest *Web Platform Components*, click **No**.

Figure 10-4
The Internet Information Services (IIS) Manager page

4. Expand the **SERVER01** node, expand **Sites**, and then expand the **Exchange Back End** node.

Question 7	*Which option allows you to specify the digital certificate and port that a website uses?*

5. Click the **Microsoft-Server-ActiveSync** node.

6. In the middle pane, under *IIS*, double-click **SSL Settings**.

7. In the middle pane, under *SSL Settings*, confirm that **Require SSL** is selected, and then click **Apply**.

8. Take a screen shot of the *Internet Information Services (IIS) Manager SSL Settings page* by pressing **Alt+PrtScr** and then paste it into your Lab 10 worksheet file in the page provided by pressing **Ctrl+V**.

9. Close **Internet Information Services (IIS) Manager**.

End of exercise. Log off Server01.

Exercise 10.6	Syncing Your Computer
Overview	In this exercise, you will create a shared folder on a server and then configure a workstation to cache those files in an offline folder.
Mindset	When a computer is not connected to the network, the user will not be able to access files that are stored on a shared folder. If you want users to access a shared folder when offline, you can sync the files.
Completion time	30 minutes

1. On *Server02*, log on using the **contoso\administrator** account and the **Pa$$word** password.

2. On the taskbar, click the **File Explorer** button to open *File Explorer*. Click **This PC** and then double-click **Local Disk (C:)**.

3. Right-click **Local Disk (C:)** in the left pane and choose **New > Folder**. For the folder name, type **Sales** and then press **Enter**.

4. Right-click the **Sales** folder and choose **Properties**.

5. Click the **Sharing** tab.

6. Click the **Advanced Sharing** button.

7. In the *Advanced Sharing* dialog box, click to select the **Share this folder** option.

8. Click the **Permissions** button.

9. In the *Permissions for Sales* dialog box, in the *Everyone* group, select **Allow Full Control**. Click **OK** to close the *Permission for Sales* dialog box.

10. Click the **Caching** button.

Question 8	*If you have confidential information that you don't want to be available on a computer that is not actively connected to the organization network, should the information folder be cached or should it not cached?*

11. Select **All files and programs that users open the shared folder are automatically available offline**.

12. Click **OK** to close the *Offline Settings* dialog box.

13. Click **OK** to close the *Advanced Sharing* dialog box.

14. Click the **Close** button to close the *Sales Properties* dialog box.

15. On *Win8A*, log on using the **contoso\administrator** account and the **Pa$$w0rd** password. On the taskbar, click **Desktop** and then click the **File Explorer** icon to open *File Explorer*.

16. Using **File Explorer**, navigate to **\\server02**.

17. Right-click the **Sales** folder and choose **Always available offline**.

18. Take a screen shot of the *server02* window by pressing **Alt+PrtScr** and then paste it into your Lab 10 worksheet file in the page provided by pressing **Ctrl+V**.

19. Double-click the **Sales** folder.

20. Right-click the empty white space of the *Sales* folder and choose **New > Text Document**.

21. Name the document **test.txt**.

22. In the top-left corner of the *Sales* folder, click the white document that displays a red checkbox icon.

23. In the *Sales (\\server02) Properties* dialog box, click the **Offline Files** tab.

24. Click the **Sync now** button.

25. Click **OK** to close the *Sales Properties* dialog box.

26. Close the **Sales** folder.

27. On the taskbar, right-click the **Network Status** icon and choose **Open Network and Sharing Center**.

28. Click **Change adapter settings**.

29. In the *Network Connections* window, right-click **Ethernet 2** and choose **Disable**.

30. On the taskbar, click the **File Explorer** button to open *File Explorer*.

31. Open the **\\server02\sales** folder.

32. Open the **test.txt** document. Type your name into the document and then save and close the document.

33. Go back to the *Network Connections* folder. Right-click **Local Area Connection** and choose **Enable**.

34. In the top-left corner of the *Sales* folder, click the white document that displays a red checkbox icon.

35. In the *Sales Properties* dialog box, click the **Offline Files** tab.

36. Click the **Sync now** button.

37. Take a screen shot of the *Sales (\\server02 Properties* window by pressing **Alt+PrtScr** and then paste it into your Lab 10 worksheet file in the page provided by pressing **Ctrl+V**.

38. Click **OK** to close the *Sales (\\server02) Properties* dialog box.

39. Double-click the **test.txt** file and observe that your name has been synced into the *Sales* folder copy of test.txt. Close the **test.txt** file.

40. Close the **Sales** folder.

End of exercise. Close the *Network Connections* folder and the *Network and Sharing Center* on Win8A.

Exercise 10.7	Using a Work Folder
Overview	In this exercise, you will create a Work Folder on Server03, and then configure a workstation to access the Work Folder.
Mindset	Work Folders allow users to store and access work files on a sync share from multiple devices including personal computers and devices (including bring-your-own devices). Work Folders are for only individual data and do not support sharing files between users.
Completion time	25 minutes

1. On *Server03*, log on using the **contoso\administrator** account and the **Pa$$w0rd** password. Using **Server Manager**, click **Manage > Add Roles and Features**.

2. In the *Add Role and Features Wizard*, on the *Before you begin* page, click **Next**.

3. On the *Select installation type* page, click **Next**.

4. On the *Select destination server* page, click **Next**.

5. On the *Select server roles* page, select the **File and Storage Services\File and iSCSI Services\Work Folders**.

6. When you are prompted to confirm that you want to install additional features, click **Add Features**.

7. Back on the *Select server roles* page, click **Next**.

8. On the *Select features* page, click **Next**.

9. On the *Confirm installation selections* page, click **Install**.

10. When the installation succeeds, click **Close**.

11. Using *Server Manager*, click **File and Storage Services**, and then click **Work Folders**, as shown in Figure 10-5.

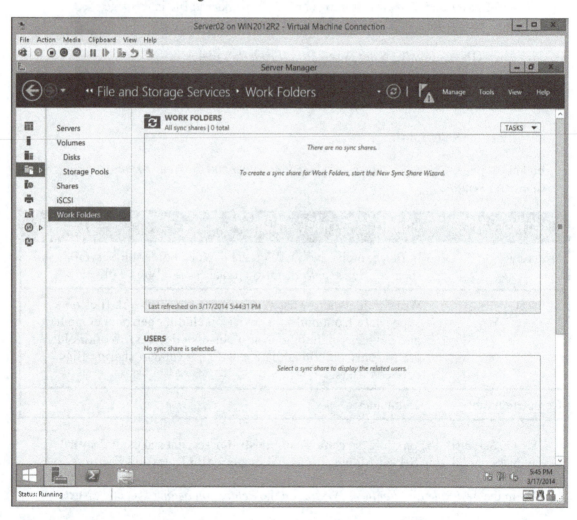

Figure 10-5
Opening the Work Folders page

12. Open **File Explorer**. Create a folder called **C:\CorpData** and then close **File Explorer**.

13. On the *Work Folders* page, click the **To create a sync share for Work Folders, start the New Sync Share Wizard** link.

14. In the **New Sync Share Wizard**, on the *Before you begin* page, click **Next**.

15. On the *Select the server and path* page, under *Enter a local path:*, browse to the **C:\CorpData** folder, and then click **Select folder**. Click **Next**.

16. On the *Specify the structure for user folders* page, with *User alias* already selected, click **Next**.

17. On the *Enter the sync share name* page, click **Next**.

18. On the *Grant sync access to groups* page, click **Add**. In the *Select User or Group* dialog box, in the *Enter the object name to select* box, type **Domain Users** and then click **OK**. Back on the *Grant sync access to groups* page, click **Next**.

19. On the *Specify device policies* page, click **Next**.

20. On the *Confirm selections* page, click **Create**.

21. Take a screen shot of the *New Sync Share Wizard* window by pressing **Alt+PrtScr** and then paste it into your Lab 10 worksheet file in the page provided by pressing **Ctrl+V**.

22. When the sync share is created, click **Close**.

23. On *Win8A*, to allow unsecure connections (http) with Work Folders, open a command prompt and execute the following command:

```
Reg add
HKLM\Software\Microsoft\Windows\CurrentVersion\WorkFol
ders /v AllowUnsecureConnection /t REG_DWORD /d 1
```

24. Close the command prompt.

25. Open the **Control Panel**, click **System and Security**, and then click **Work Folders**.

26. On the manage *Work Folders* page, click **Set up Work Folders**.

Question 9	You have defined Work Folders on multiple servers for 100s of users. What is the easiest way to automatically set up Work Folders for your users?

27. On the *Enter your work email address* page, click **Enter a Work Folders URL instead**.

28. On the *Enter a Work Folders URL* page, in the Work Folders URL text box, type **http://server03.contoso.com** and then click **Next**.

29. On the *Introducing Work Folders* page, click **Next**.

30. On the *Security policies* page, select **I accept these policies on my PC** and then click **Set up Work Folders**.

31. Click **Close**.

32. Close the **Work Folders** window.

33. Take a screen shot of the Control Panel's *Work Folders* window by pressing **Alt+PrtScr** and then paste it into your Lab 10 worksheet file in the page provided by pressing **Ctrl+V**.

34. Close **Control Panel**.

End of exercise. Log off the system.

Lab Challenge	Performing a Mobile Device Remote Wipe
Overview	To complete this challenge, you must demonstrate how to view mobile devices assigned to an Exchange user account and how to wipe a phone.
Mindset	You are an administrator for the Contoso Corporation and a user is leaving the company. Therefore, you want to see the mobile devices assigned to the user so you can remotely wipe the phone by using the Outlook Web App (OWA) and by using the Exchange Control Panel (ECP).
Completion time	10 minutes

Write out the steps you need to perform in order to complete this challenge.

To use the Outlook Web App (OWA), perform the following steps:

To use the Exchange Control Panel (ECP), perform the following steps:

End of lab.

LAB 11
MANAGING ENDPOINT SECURITY

THIS LAB CONTAINS THE FOLLOWING EXERCISES AND ACTIVITIES:

BEFORE YOU BEGIN

The lab environment consists of student workstations connected to a local area network, along with a server that functions as the domain controller for a domain called contoso.com. The computers required for this lab are listed in Table 11-1.

Table 11-1
Computers Required for Lab 11

Computer	Operating System	Computer Name
Server	Windows Server 2012 R2	RWDC01
Server	Windows Server 2012 R2	Server02
Client	Windows 8	Win8B

In addition to the computers, you will also need the software listed in Table 11-2 to complete Lab 11.

Table 11-2
Software Required for Lab 11

Software	Location
Lab 11 student worksheet	Lab11_worksheet.docx (provided by instructor)

Working with Lab Worksheets

Each lab in this manual requires that you answer questions, shoot screen shots, and perform other activities that you will document in a worksheet named for the lab, such as Lab11_worksheet.docx. You will find these worksheets on the book companion site. It is recommended that you use a USB flash drive to store your worksheets so you can submit them to your instructor for review. As you perform the exercises in each lab, open the appropriate worksheet file, fill in the required information, and then save the file to your flash drive.

SCENARIO

After completing this lab, you will be able to:

■ Install and configure Windows Server Update Services (WSUS)

■ Install updates to a client using WSUS

■ Approve updates

■ Configure functionality of Group Policy Objects

■ Configure blocking inheritance and enforced policies

■ Configure security filtering and WMI filtering

■ Configuring loopback processing

■ Schedule a scan using Windows Defender scan

Estimated lab time: 125 minutes

Exercise 11.1	Installing Windows Server Update Services (WSUS)
Overview	In this exercise, you will use Server Manager to install WSUS. Because this is a test environment, you will use the standard internal database that comes with Windows.
Mindset	When planning WSUS, you must consider several factors when deciding which server to place the WSUS role on. You should consider the number of clients, the number of updates, the location of the clients, the bandwidth links between the clients and the WSUS server, and the available disk space. If you have multiple sites, you might consider installing multiple WSUS servers within your organization so that you can preserve WAN bandwidth. You can then consider using a WSUS architecture.
Completion time	25 minutes

1. On *RWDC01*, log on using the **contoso\administrator** account and the **Pa$$w0rd** password.

2. On the taskbar, click the **File Explorer** icon and navigate to the **Local Disk (C:)** drive.

3. Right-click the white space of the *Local Disk (C:)* window and choose **New > Folder**. For the folder name, type **Updates** and then click **Enter**.

   To deploy WSUS, Network Services must have Full Control to the %windir%\Microsoft.NET\Framework\v2.0.50727\Temporary ASP.NET Files and %windir%\Temp folder. Therefore, the new few steps change permissions for the %windir%Temp folder.

4. First, open the **%windir%** folder.

Question 1	What directory is the %windir% folder?

5. Right-click the **Temp** folder and choose **Properties**.

6. In the *Temp Properties* dialog box, click the **Security** tab.

7. Click the **Edit** button (see Figure 11-1).

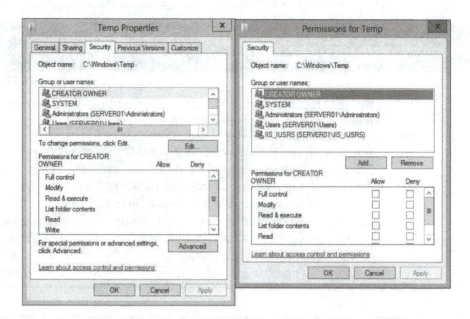

Figure 11-1
Accessing the Permissions for the Temp folder

8. In the *Permissions for Temp* folder, click **Add**.

9. In the *Select Users, Computers, Service Accounts, or Groups* dialog box, in the *Enter the object names to select* text box, type **network service** and then click **Enter**.

10. While *NETWORK SERVICE* is selected, for the *Full control* setting, click to select the **Allow**.

11. Take a screen shot of the *Permissions for Temp* dialog box by pressing **Alt+PrtScr** and then paste it into your Lab 11 worksheet file in the page provided by pressing **Ctrl+V**.

12. Click **OK** to close the *Permissions for Temp* dialog box. If you are prompted to confirm that you want to change the permissions settings on system folders, click **Yes**.

13. Click **OK** to close the *Temp Properties* dialog box.

14. If *Server Manager* is not open, open **Server Manager**.

15. At the top of *Server Manager*, click **Manage > Add Roles and Features**. The *Add Roles and Feature Wizard* displays.

16. On the *Before you begin* page, click **Next**.

17. Select **Role-based or feature-based installation** and then click **Next**.

18. On the *Select destination server* page, click **Next**.

19. Scroll down and select **Windows Server Update Services**.

20. On the *Add Roles and Features Wizard* page, click **Add Features**.

21. Back on the *Select server roles* screen, click **Next**.

22. On the *Select features* page, click **Next**.

23. On the *Windows Server Update Services* page, click **Next**.

24. By default, the *WID database* and *WSUS Services* are selected. Answer the following question and then click **Next**.

Question 2	Which option would you pick to store the database on a dedicated SQL server?

25. In the *Store updates in the following location* text box, type **C:\Updates** and then click **Next**.

26. On the *Web Server Role (IIS)* page, click **Next**.

27. On the *Select role services* page, click **Next**.

NOTE	Remember, if this was a production environment, you would store the updates on a non-system drive.

28. On the *Confirm installation selections* page, click **Install**.

29. When the installation has finished, take a screen shot of the *Installation progress* screen by pressing **Alt+PrtScr** and then paste it into your Lab 11 worksheet file in the page provided by pressing **Ctrl+V**.

30. When the installation has finished, click **Close**.

End of exercise. Leave any windows open for the next exercise.

Exercise 11.2	Configuring WSUS
Overview	After you install WSUS, you must configure WSUS so that it retrieves updates from Microsoft or another WSUS server. You also must configure WSUS to identify the updates that need to be downloaded and when those downloads should occur.
Mindset	When you configure the WSUS server, you need to pull down a list of available updates from the Microsoft Update website or another Windows Update server. You also have to organize the computers into groups. When you deploy updates, you deploy to the groups.
Completion time	20 minutes

1. On *RWDC01*, if *Server Manager* is not open, open **Server Manager**.

2. At the top of the *Server Manager* window, click **Tools > Windows Server Update Services**.

3. In the *Complete WSUS Installation* dialog box (see Figure 11-2), click **Run**.

Figure 11-2
Completing WSUS installation

4. When the post-installation has finished, click **Close**.

5. On the *Before You Begin* page, click **Next**.

6. On the *Join the Microsoft Update Improvement Program* page, click **Next**. The *Choose Upstream Server* page displays.

7. Click **Synchronize from another Windows Server Update Services server**. In the *Server name* text box, type **server02.contoso.com**. Answer the following question and then click **Next**.

Question 3	*If you synchronize from another WSUS server, what is the default port used?*

8. On the *Specify Proxy Server* page, click **Next**.

9. On the *Connect to Upstream Server* page, click **Start Connecting**.

10. When the connection is complete, click **Next**.

11. On the *Choose Languages* page, choose one language that you need to support and then click **Next**.

NOTE	*If you were updating directly from Microsoft, you would choose which products and which classifications to download. However, because you are downloading from another WSUS server, you automatically get the products and classifications used on the upstream server.*

12. On the *Set Sync Schedule* page, click **Next**.

13. On the *Finished* page, select **Begin initial synchronization** and then click **Next**.

14. On the *What's Next* page, click **Finish**.

15. On the *Update Services* console, expand **RWDC01** and then click **Synchronizations**.

16. Wait until the initial synchronization finishes. You can update the screen by pressing the **F5** key or by right-clicking **Synchronizations** and choosing **Refresh**.

17. Right-click **Synchronizations** and choose **Synchronization Now** (if needed).

18. Take a screen shot of the *Update Services* console by pressing **Alt+PrtScr** and then paste it into your Lab 11 worksheet file in the page provided by pressing **Ctrl+V**.

19. Go to the *Update Services* console. At the bottom of the left pane, click **Options** to show the WSUS options. View the available options.

20. In the left pane, expand **Computers** so that you can see **All Computers**.

21. Right-click **All Computers** and choose **Add Computer Group**. The *Add Computer Group* dialog box opens.

22. In the *Name* text box, type **Group1**. Click **Add** to apply your settings and to close the *Add Computer Group* dialog box.

End of exercise. Leave any windows open for the next exercise.

Exercise 11.3	Configuring WSUS Clients
Overview	For a client to get updates from a WSUS, the client has to be configured to get updates from WSUS. Therefore, in this exercise, you will use Group Policy Objects (GPOs) to configure Server02 to get updates from Server01.
Mindset	To configure a client to get updates from a WSUS server, you should use group policies so that it can automatically specify WSUS settings for a client. You can use GPOs to configure where to get the updates, when installations will be installed, and which Computer Group the computer will be added to.
Completion time	15 minutes

1. On *RWDC01*, using *Server Manager*, click **Tools > Active Directory Users and Computers**. The *Active Directory Users and Computers* console opens.

2. Right-click **CONTOSO.COM** and choose **New > Organizational Unit**. In the *Name* text box, type **Updates** and then click **OK**.

3. Navigate to and click the **Computers** container.

4. Right-click **Win8B** and choose **Move**.

5. Select **Updates** and then click **OK**.

6. Close **Active Directory Users and Computers**.

7. With *Server Manager*, click **Tools > Group Policy Management**. The *Group Policy Management* console opens.

8. In the tree structure (left pane), navigate to and click **Updates** in the *contoso.com* domain.

9. Right-click **Updates** and choose **Create a GPO in this domain, and Link it here**.

10. In the *New GPO* dialog box, in the *Name* text box, type **Computer Updates** and then click **OK**.

11. Right-click **Computer Updates GPO** and choose **Edit**. The *Group Policy Management Editor* opens.

12. In the *Group Policy Management Editor* window, expand **Computer Configuration > Policies > Administrative Templates > Windows Components** and then click **Windows Update**.

13. In the details pane, double-click **Specify Intranet Microsoft update service location**. The *Specify intranet Microsoft update service location* page displays.

14. Select **Enabled**.

15. In the *Set the intranet update service for detecting updates* text box and in the *Set the intranet statistics server* text box, type **HTTP://RWDC01:8053**.

16. Click **OK** to apply your settings and to close the *Specify intranet Microsoft update service location* page.

17. In the details pane, double-click **Enable client-side targeting**. The *Enable client-side targeting* page appears.

18. Select **Enabled** and in the *Target group name for this computer* text box, type **Group1**.

Question 4	What is the maximum number of groups that a client computer can be in?

19. Click **OK** to apply your settings and to close the *Enable client-side targeting* page.

20. Take a screen shot of the *Group Policy Management Editor* window that shows the two settings enabled by pressing **Alt+PrtScr** and then paste it into your Lab 11 worksheet file in the page provided by pressing **Ctrl+V**.

Question 5	If you don't use a GPO to configure clients to use WSUS, how would you configure the system?

End of exercise. Leave any windows open for the next exercise.

Exercise 11.4	Approving Updates
Overview	The WSUS server has been configured and you have a client that is ready to get updates from the WSUS server. In this exercise, you will approve what updates need to be pushed.
Mindset	One of the primary advantages of using WSUS to deploy updates is that you can control which updates are deployed and you can specify when the updates get deployed. By controlling the updates, you can test each update before it is deployed to an organization to ensure it will not cause any problems for the users of the organization.
Completion time	10 minutes

1. On *RWDC01*, go to the **Update Services** console.

2. In the left pane, under the *RWDC01* node, expand the **Updates** node. Then click the **Updates** node (see Figure 11-3).

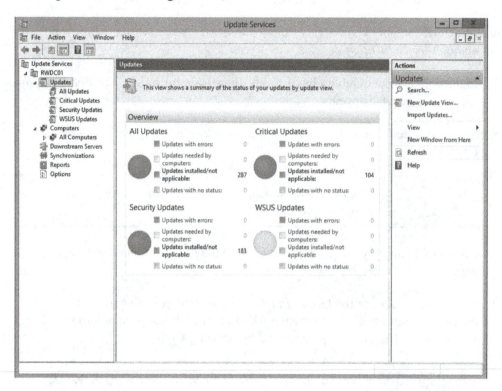

Figure 11-3
The Update Services node

3. Click **Critical Updates**.

4. On the top of the screen, on the *Approval* drop-down, make sure **Unapproved** is selected. On the top of the screen, on the *Status* drop-down menu, ensure **Any** is selected.

5. Click **Refresh** to display the updates.

6. To click several updates, hold the **Ctrl** key and click several updates. When you're finished selecting your updates, release the **Ctrl** key.

7. Right-click one of the selected updates and choose **Approve**.

8. If the *Approve Updates* dialog box displays, right-click **Group1** and then choose **Approved For Install**. Click **OK**.

9. If a license agreement displays, prompting you for an update, click **I Accept**.

10. Take a screen shot of the *Approval Progress* dialog box by pressing **Alt+PrtScr** and then paste it into your Lab 11 worksheet file in the page provided by pressing **Ctrl+V**.

11. Click **Close** to close the *Approval Progress* dialog box.

Question 6	*How would you configure to automatically approve updates?*

End of exercise. Close all open windows.

Exercise 11.5	Configuring Processing and Precedence of Group Policy Objects
Overview	In this exercise, you will create multiple GPOs and look at overall precedence of the GPOs.
Mindset	Group policies are applied from top to bottom. In general, when a GPO is executed after an earlier executed GPO, the GPO executed later overwrites conflicting settings. If there is more than one GPO at a level, each GPO will be processed as specified by the precedence level.
Completion time	20 minutes

1. Using *Server Manager*, click **Tools > Active Directory Users and Computers**. The *Active Directory Users and Computers* console opens.

2. If the *Sales* OU is not created, create the **Sales** OU.

3. Under the *Sales* OU, create an **East** OU and a **West** OU.

4. Using *Server Manager*, click **Tools > Group Policy Management**. The *Group Policy Management* console opens.

5. Navigate to and click the **Sales** OU.

6. Right-click the **Sales** OU and choose **Create a GPO in this domain, and Link it here**. In the *New GPO* dialog box, type in **GPO1** and then click **OK**.

7. Create a GPO called **GPO2** for *West* OU.

8. Create a GPO called **GPO3** for the *East* OU.

9. Create a GPO called **GPO4** for the *contoso.com* domain.

10. Create a GPO called **GPO5** for the *Sales* OU.

11. Create a GPO called **GPO6** for the *East* OU.

12. Create a GPO called **GPO7** for the *East* OU.

13. Click **East**, as shown in Figure 11-4. In the *East* pane, click **Group Policy Inheritance**.

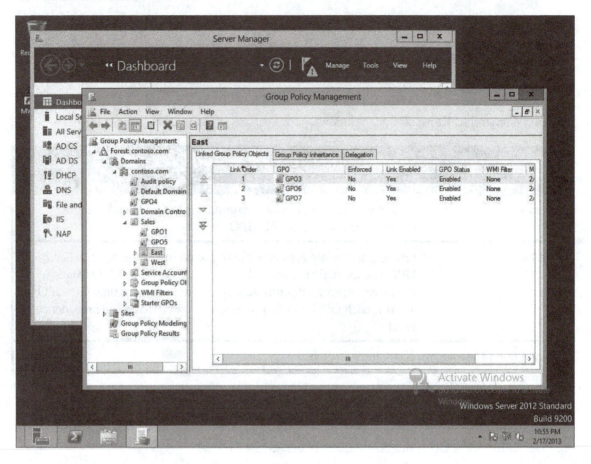

Figure 11-4
Viewing GPOs linked to a OU

Question 7	*What is the order of GPOs that are being applied?*

14. For the *East* OU, click **Linked Group Policy Objects**.

Question 8	*What are the three GPOs linked to the East OU? List them in order.*

15. Click **GPO7**. Then click the double up arrow.

Question 9	*What are the three GPOs linked to the East OU? List them in order.*

16. Click the **Group Policy Inheritance** tab.

Question 10	*What is the order of GPOs that are being applied?*

17. Take a screen shot of the *Group Policy Management* window by pressing
    Alt+PrtScr and then paste it into your Lab 11 worksheet file in the page
    provided by pressing **Ctrl+V**.

End of exercise. Leave the *Group Policy Management* console open for the next
exercise.

Exercise 11.6	Configuring Blocking Inheritance and Enforced Policies
Overview	In this exercise, you will modify the order and precedence of GPOs by blocking inheritance and using enforced policies.
Mindset	If you want group policies to stop inheriting, you can actually use block inheritance. If you want to ensure that a group policy is not overwritten, you can select enforced.
Completion time	10 minutes

1. On *RWDC01*, using *Group Policy Management*, navigate to and click the
   East OU.

2. Right-click the **East** OU and choose **Block Inheritance**. An exclamation point
   inside a blue circle appears for the *East* container, as shown in Figure 11-5.

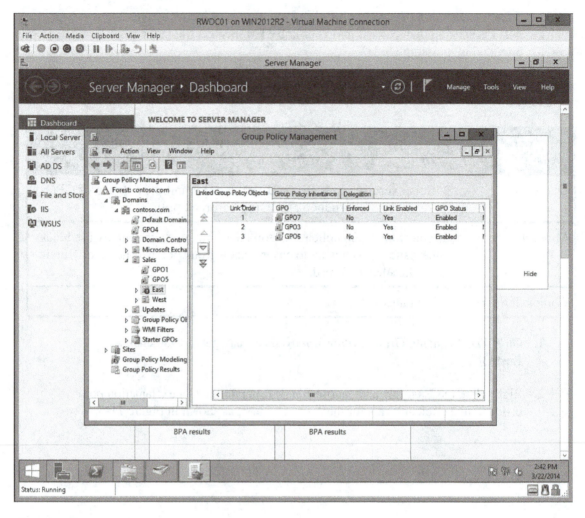

Figure 11-5
Viewing the East OU with block inheritance

3. Click the **Group Policy Inheritance** tab.

Question 11	What is the order of GPOs that are being applied to the East OU?

4. Under *contoso.com*, right-click **GPO4** and choose **Enforced**.

Question 12	What is the order of GPOs that are being applied to the East OU? Note: You might need to press F5 to refresh the screen.

5. Take a screen shot of the *Group Policy Management* window by pressing **Alt+PrtScr** and then paste it into your Lab 11 worksheet file in the page provided by pressing **Ctrl+V**.

End of exercise. Leave the Group Policy Management console open for the next exercise.

Exercise 11.7	Configuring Security Filtering and WMI Filtering
Overview	In this exercise, you will fine-tune the processing of GPOs by using security filtering and WMI filtering.
Mindset	You can use security filtering and WMI filtering to give you control of how GPOs are applied. Security filtering allows you to define groups and users and their associated permissions for a GPO. WMI filtering allows you to look for certain parameters on the computer that they are running such as a particular operating system or a certain type of hardware.
Completion time	10 minutes

1. On *RWDC01*, using *Server Manager*, click **Tools > Active Directory Users and Computers**.

2. In the *Active Directory Users and Computers* console, under *Contoso.com*, right-click the **Sales** OU and choose **New > User**.

3. In the *New Object – User* dialog box, type the following information and click Next:

   First name: **John**

   Last name: **Smith**

   User logon name: **JSmith**

4. In the *Password* text box and the *Confirm password* text box, type **Pa$$w0rd**.

5. Click **Password never expires**. When a warning appears, click **OK** and then click **Next**.

6. When the wizard is complete, click **Finish**.

7. Using *Group Policy Management*, click the **GPO5** that is assigned to the *Sales* OU. If necessary, click **OK** in the message box that appears.

8. Click the **Delegation** tab and then click **Advanced**. The *GPO5 Security Settings* dialog box opens, as shown in Figure 11-6.

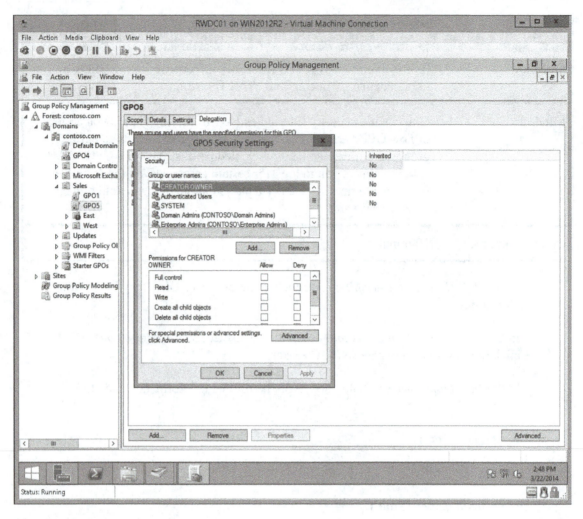

Figure 11-6
Viewing a GPO security settings

Question 13	What permissions are needed for a GPO to apply to a user?

9. Click the **Add** button. The *Select users, Computers, Service Accounts, or Groups* dialog box opens.

10. In the text box, type **John Smith** and then click **Enter**.

11. With **John Smith** highlighted, assign the **Deny Apply** group policy and then click **OK**. When a message indicates that *Deny entries take precedence* and prompts you to confirm that you want to continue, click **Yes**.

12. In the left pane, navigate to and click **WMI filters**.

13. Right-click the **WMI Filters** node and choose **New**. The *New WMI Filter* dialog box opens, as shown in Figure 11-7.

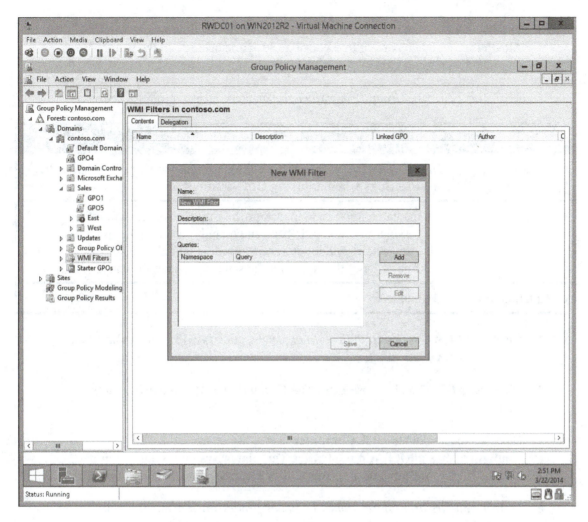

Figure 11-7
Creating a new WMI filter

14. In the *Name* text box, type **WMIFilter1**.

15. In the *Queries* section, click **Add**. The *WMI Query* dialog box opens.

16. In the *Query* text box, type the following and then click **OK**:

    ```
    Select * from Win32_Processor where AddressWidth ='32'
    ```

    When you are prompted to confirm you want to use this namespace, click **OK**.

17. Click **Save** to create the WMI filter.

18. Click **GPO5**. If a message box appears, click **OK**. Click the **Scope** tab.

19. Under WMI Filtering, select **WMIFilter1**. Click **Yes** to confirm your changes.

20. Take a screen shot of the *Group Policy Management* window by pressing **Alt+PrtScr** and then paste it into your Lab 11 worksheet file in the page provided by pressing **Ctrl+V**.

End of exercise. Leave the *Group Policy Management* console open for the next exercise.

Exercise 11.8	Configuring Loopback Processing
Overview	In this exercise, you will have the computer settings overwrite the user settings when applying GPO settings.
Mindset	As the name implies, loopback processing allows the Group Policy processing order to circle back and reapply the computer policies after all user policies and logon scripts run. It is intended to keep the configuration of the computer the same regardless of who logs on.
Completion time	5 minutes

1. On *RWDC01*, using *Group Policy Management*, click **GPO1**. If a message box appears, click **OK**.

2. Right-click **GPO1** and choose **Edit**. The *Group Policy Management Editor* opens.

3. Navigate to and double-click **Computer Configuration\Policies\Administrative Templates\System\Group Policy**. Double-click **Configure user Group Policy Loopback processing mode**.

4. In the *Configure user Group Policy loopback processing mode* dialog box, click **Enabled**.

Question 14	What is the difference between Replace and Merge?

5. Change the mode to **Merge**.

6. Take a screen shot of the *Configure user Group Policy loopback processing mode* window by pressing **Alt+PrtScr** and then paste it into your Lab 11 worksheet file in the page provided by pressing **Ctrl+V**.

7. Click **OK**.

8. Close **Group Policy Management Editor**.

End of exercise. Close all windows on Win8B.

Lab Challenge	Scheduling Windows Defender Scan
Overview	To complete this challenge, you must demonstrate how to schedule Windows Defender Scan.
Mindset	In Windows 8, Windows Defender is used to protect a computer against malware. Without Windows Defender or similar software, your computer is vulnerable to viruses, worms, Trojans, and other security breaches.
Completion time	10 minutes

Write out the steps you need to perform in order to complete the challenge. When you have completed the scheduling activity, take a screen shot of the Windows Defender Scheduled Scan dialog box and paste it into your Lab 11 worksheet file.

End of lab.

LAB 12
USING WINDOWS INTUNE TO MANAGE CLIENTS

THIS LAB CONTAINS THE FOLLOWING EXERCISES AND ACTIVITIES:

Exercise 12.1	Deploying the Windows Intune Client
Exercise 12.2	Creating a Device Group Using Direct Membership
Exercise 12.3	Managing Updates with Windows Intune
Exercise 12.4	Running Windows Intune Reports
Exercise 12.5	Managing Policies
Exercise 12.6	Managing Intune Endpoint Protection
Exercise 12.7	Removing the Windows Intune Client
Lab Challenge	Customizing the Windows Intune Company Portal

BEFORE YOU BEGIN

Different from most of the previous labs, this lab requires the use of a computer
running Windows 8.1 that is connected to the Internet. If the computer does not have
Microsoft Silverlight, you will be asked to install Silverlight. In addition, you will be
installing the Intune client software. Therefore, you will need to have administrative
access to the computer. The computer can be a stand-alone computer running
Windows 8.1 or a virtual machine running on Hyper-V that is configured to access
the Internet.

In addition to the computer, you will also require the software listed in Table 12-1 to complete Lab 12.

Table 12-1
Software Required for Lab 12

Software	Location
Lab 12 student worksheet	Lab12_worksheet.docx (provided by instructor)

Working with Lab Worksheets

Each lab in this manual requires that you answer questions, shoot screen shots, and perform other activities that you will document in a worksheet named for the lab, such as Lab12_worksheet.docx. You will find these worksheets on the book companion site. It is recommended that you use a USB flash drive to store your worksheets so you can submit them to your instructor for review. As you perform the exercises in each lab, open the appropriate worksheet file, fill in the required information, and then save the file to your flash drive.

SCENARIO

After completing this lab, you will be able to:

- Deploy the Windows Intune Client

- Create a device group using direct membership

- Manage updates and update groups using Windows Intune

- Run Windows Intune reports

- Manage policies

- Manage Intune Endpoint Protection

- Configure the Windows Intune company portal

Estimated lab time: 105 minutes

> **NOTE**
>
> *If you are using MOAC Labs Online, you will not be able to perform this lab using an online computer. Instead, you will need use a computer running Windows 8.1 with access to the Internet. If your classroom has a dedicated Windows Server 2012 R2 for each user, you can use a virtual machine running Windows 8.1.*

Exercise12.1	Deploying the Windows Intune Client
Overview	In this exercise, you will deploy the Windows Intune client to your local computer or a virtual machine that is running Windows 8.1 and has access to the Internet. If you are using MOAC Labs Online, you will not be able to perform this lab using an online computer. Instead, you will need use a computer running Windows 8 with access to the Internet. If your classroom has a dedicated Windows Server 2012 R2 for each user, you can use a virtual machine running Windows 8.1.
Mindset	Windows Intune is a cloud-based service provided by Microsoft that allows you to manage clients within your organization, including deploying updates.
Completion time	25 minutes

1. On *Win8A*, log on using the **contoso\administrator** account and the **Pa$$w0rd** password.

2. On the *Start* screen, click **Internet Explorer**.

3. Go to **http://www.microsoft.com/en-us/windows/windowsintune/try.aspx**.

4. Scroll down and click **Sign up for a free Windows Intune 30-day trial**.

5. On the signup page, type the following information:

   Country or Region: **<Your country or region>**

   Organization language: **<Your language>**

   First Name: **<Your first name>**

   Last Name: **<Your last name>**

   Organization: **<Your last name> Corporation**

   Address: **<Your street address>**

   City: **<Your city>**

   State: **<Your state>**

   Zip code: **<Your zip code>**

   Phone number: **<Your phone number>**

   Email address: **<Your email address>**

6. In the *New domain name* text box, type the following:

    <FirstName><LastName>Training<Month><Year>

    Therefore, if your name is John Smith and you are performing this lab in June 2014, you would type the following:

    JohnSmithTraining062014 in front of *.onmicrosoft.com*

Question 1	What is the name of the account you are creating?

7. Click **Check availability**.

8. In the *New user ID* text box, type your first initial and last name. Therefore, if your name is John Smith, type *JSmith*.

9. For the *Create new password* text box and the *Confirm new password* text box, type **Pa$$w0rd**.

10. In the *Verification* text box, type the code displayed.

11. Click **I accept and continue**.

12. Click **Continue**.

13. If a *Windows Intune login* screen appears, in the *Password* text box, type **Pa$$w0rd** and then click **Sign in**.

14. If a *Don't lose access to your account* displays, click **Remind me later**.

15. Press **Alt+Prt Scr** to take a screen shot of the *Windows Intune Admin Overview* page. Press **Ctrl+V** to paste the image on the page provided in the Lab 12 worksheet file.

16. On the *Windows Intune Admin Overview* screen, in the menu bar just below the webpage address, click **Admin Console**.

17. If a message appears, indicating the application requires Microsoft Silverlight, click **Get Microsoft Silverlight**. When you are prompted to run or save *Silverlight_x64.exe*, click **Run**. If the User Account Control dialog box displays, click **Yes**.

18. In the *Install Silverlight* dialog box, click **Install now**. When you are prompted to enable *Microsoft Update*, click **Next**. Click **Close**.

19. If you are prompted to log in, type **Pa$$w0rd** in the *Password* text box.

20. On the *System Overview* page, click **Download and Deploy the Client Software**.

21. In the *Step 2: Download and Deploy* section, click **Download Client Software**.

22. When you are prompted to indicate what you want to do with *Windows_Intune_Setup.zip*, click **Save**. Click Save to save it in the folder.

23. When the download has finished, click **Open folder**.

Question 2	*Which folder was the zip file saved to?*

24. Double-click the **Windows_Intune_Setup.zip** file.

25. Double-click the **Windows_Intune_Setup.exe** application.

26. In the *Compressed (zipped) Folders* dialog box, click **Run**.

27. On the *Windows Intune Setup Wizard* page, click **Next**. If prompted to allow installation, click **Yes**.

28. When Windows Intune client is installed, click **Finish**.

Windows Intune continues to update and install software on the computer. You can use the computer while the process continues in the background.

29. Close the *Windows_Intune_Setup* window, if needed.

30. Using **Internet Explorer**, in the *Windows Intune* window, click **Overview**.

31. Press **Alt+Prt Scr** to take a screen shot of the *Administration Overview* page. Press **Ctrl+V** to paste the image on the page provided in the Lab 12 worksheet file.

End of exercise. Leave the *Administration Overview* page open for the next exercise.

Exercise 12.2	Creating a Device Group Using Direct Membership
Overview	In this exercise, you will create a Windows Intune group that will be used to organize your resources.
Mindset	As you can do with Active Directory groups, you can assign devices to groups and then apply updates directly to a group.
Completion time	10 minutes

1. On the *Administration Overview* page, in the far-left column of icons, click the **Groups** icon (second from the top).

2. Under the *Tasks* menu, click **Create Group**.

3. In the *Group name* field, type **My Test Group**.

4. In the *Description* field, type **Computers used to test deployments of new updates**.

5. Under the *Select a parent* group, click **All Devices**.

6. Click **Next**.

7. On the *Criteria Membership* page, click **Next**.

8. On the *Direct Membership* page, next to the *Include specific members* section, click **Browse**.

9. Click your Windows 8.1 computer and then click **Add**. Your Windows 8.1 computer should appear in the *Include specific members* column. Click **OK** to continue.

10. On the *Direct Membership* page, click **Next**.

11. On the *Summary* page, review the Ge*neral Criteria Membership* and *Direct Membership* information and then click **Finish**.

12. When the group is created, press **Ctrl+PrtScr** to take a screen shot of the *My Test Group* page. Press **Ctrl+V** to paste the image on the page provided in the Lab 12 worksheet file.

13. Answer Question 3. Then under *Groups, All Devices*, click **My Test Group** and then click **Devices**. The computer should appear as a member of the group.

Question 3	Do any devices have alerts?

14. Press **Ctrl+PrtScr** to take a screen shot of the *My Test Group* page with the computer shown. Press **Ctrl+V** to paste the image on the page provided in the Lab 12 worksheet file.

End of exercise. Leave the *Windows Intune* page open for the next exercise.

Exercise 12.3	Managing Updates with Windows Intune
Overview	In this exercise, you will approve updates for Windows Intune clients.
Mindset	Similar to deploying updates with WSUS, you can deploy updates with Windows Intune. By controlling which updates are deployed and when they're deployed, you can test updates before they are deployed.
Completion time	20 minutes

1. On the *Windows Intune* page
   (*https://manage.microsoft.com/windowsintune/app.aspx*), in the far-left column,
   click the **Updates** icon (the third icon from the top). The *Updates Overview* page
   displays (see Figure 12-1).

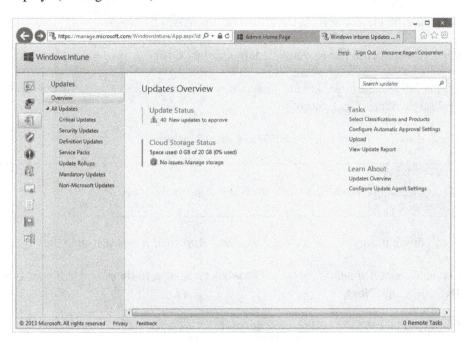

Figure 12-1
The Updates Overview page

2. Click **# New updates to approve**. (The actual number of updates to approve will
   vary according to the number of updates Microsoft has posted since your last
   update.)

3. Right-click the first update and choose **Approve**.

4. Normally, you would select the group for which you want to install the update.
   Since we will not be installing updates, click **Ungrouped devices** to demonstrate
   how to set up how to unapprove an update. Click **Add**.

5. Click **Next**.

6. On the *Deployment Action* page, click **Do Not Install** and then click **Required
   Install**.

7. Press **Alt+Prt Scr** to take a screen shot of the *Deployment Action* page. Press
   Ctrl+V to paste the image on the page provided in the Lab 12 worksheet file.

8. Click **Finish**.

9. To decline an update, right-click the same update and choose **Decline**. In the
   Decline dialog box, click **Decline**.

10. Press **Alt+Prt Scr** to take a screen shot of the *All Updates* window. Press **Ctrl+V** to paste the image on the page provided in the Lab 12 worksheet file.

11. Click **Overview**.

12. Under *Tasks*, click **Configure Automatic Approval Settings**.

13. Click to deselect **Windows** and click to deselect **Office**.

14. On the *Service Settings: Updates* page, scroll to and click to select **Microsoft Online Services**. Click **Save**.

15. Scroll down until you can see **Update Classification**.

Question 4	Which classifications are already selected?

16. Scroll down until you can see the *Automatic Approval Rules* section. Click **New**.

17. On the *Create Automatic Approval Rule* Wizard page, in the *Name* text box, type **Default**. Click **Next**.

18. Click to select **Works** and then click **Next**.

19. On the *Update Classifications* page, click to select **Critical Updates** and then click **Next**.

20. On the *Deployment* page, click **Ungrouped Devices** and then click **Add**. Click **Next**.

21. On the *Summary* page, click **Finish**.

22. Press **Alt+Prt Scr** to take a screen shot of the *Service Settings: Updates* page. Press **Ctrl+V** to paste the image on the page provided in the Lab 12 worksheet file.

23. On the *Service Settings: Updates* page, click **Save**.

End of exercise. Leave the *Windows Intune* page open for the next exercise.

Exercise 12.4	Running Intune Reports
Overview	In this exercise, you will run update reports for Windows Intune clients, showing which updates have been selected to be deployed and which updates have been actually deployed.
Mindset	Windows Intune provides multiple reports that allow you to view the status of client devices, including updates.
Completion time	5 minutes

1. On the *Windows Intune* page (*https://manage.microsoft.com/windowsintune/app.aspx*), in the left pane, click **Reports** (the second-to-last icon). The *Reports Overview* page appears, as shown in Figure 12-2.

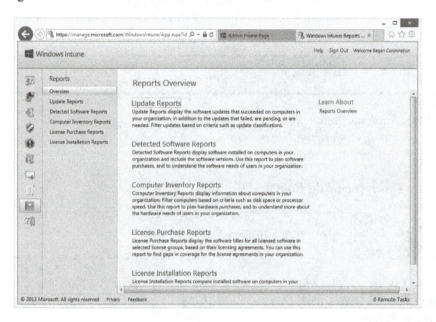

Figure 12-2
The Reports Overview page

Question 5	Which report would you use to determine the software that each device has?

2. On the *Reports Overview* page, click **Update Reports**.

3. On the *Update Reports – Create New Report* page, click **View Report**.

4. Under *Table of Contents*, click **Criteria**.

5. To rerun the same report, under *Table of Contents*, in the left pane of the screen, click the **Update Report** button.

6. Take a screen shot of the *Update Report* page by pressing **Alt+Prt Scr** and then paste it into your Lab 12 worksheet file in the page provided by pressing **Ctrl+V**.

7. Close the **Update Report** window by closing the **Internet Explorer** page.

End of exercise. Leave the *Windows Intune* page open for the next exercise.

Exercise 12.5	Managing Policies
Overview	In this exercise, you will create a Mobile Device Security Policy, and then modify the new policy that you just created.
Mindset	To help control the security settings on mobile devices, computer updates, Endpoint Protection, firewall settings, and the end-user experience, Windows Intune has policies. These policies apply to domain-joined computers in any domain and to non-domain joined computers.
Completion time	10 minutes

1. On the *Windows Intune* page (*https://manage.microsoft.com/windowsintune/app.aspx*), in the left pane, click **Policy** (the third-to-last icon).

2. Under *Tasks*, click **Add Policy**.

Question 6	Which four templates are available?

3. In the *Create a New Policy* window, *Mobile Device Security Policy* and *Create and Deploy a Policy with the Recommended Settings* are already selected. Click **Create Policy**.

4. On the *Select the groups to which you want to deploy this policy* page, click **Ungrouped Users** and then click **Add**. Click **OK**.

5. Back on the *Policies* screen click **Edit**.

6. Change the *Number of repeated sign-in failures to allow before the device is wiped* to **10**.

7. Take a screen shot of the *Edit Policy* page by pressing **Alt+PrtScr** and then paste it into your Lab 12 worksheet file in the page provided by pressing **Ctrl+V**.

8. Click **Save Policy**.

End of exercise. Leave the Windows Intune page open for the next exercise.

Exercise 12.6	Managing Intune Endpoint Protection
Overview	In this exercise, you will verify that a system is free of malware and determine how to schedule a malware scan using Windows Intune.
Mindset	To help control the security settings on mobile devices, computer updates, Endpoint Protection, firewall settings, and the end-user experience, Windows Intune has policies. These policies apply to domain-joined computers in any domain and to non-domain joined computers.
Completion time	10 minutes

1. On the *Windows Intune* page (*https://manage.microsoft.com/windowsintune/app.aspx*), in the left pane, click **Software** (the sixth icon).

2. On the *Software Overview* page, click **Detected Software**.

Question 7	What are the first three detected software packages?

3. In the left pane, click **EndPoint Protection** (the fourth icon).

Question 8	Do you have any issues?

4. Take a screen shot of the *Endpoint Protection Overview* page by pressing **Alt+PrtScr** and then paste it into your Lab 12 worksheet file in the page provided by pressing **Ctrl+V**.

5. In the *Learn About* section, click **How to Schedule a Scan**.

Question 9	How do you scan an on-demand remote scan?

End of exercise. Leave the *Windows Intune* page open for the next exercise.

Exercise 12.7	Removing the Windows Intune Client
Overview	In this exercise, you will remove the Windows Intune client that you installed in Exercise 12.1 so that the client computer is in the same state before you started this exercise.
Mindset	The client computer will no longer use Windows Intune to manage client devices, so you can remove the Windows Intune client software by using the Control Panel.
Completion time	5 minutes

1. Right-click the **Start** button and choose **Control Panel**.

2. Under the *Programs* section, click **Uninstall a program**. The *Uninstall or change a program* page appears (see Figure 12-3).

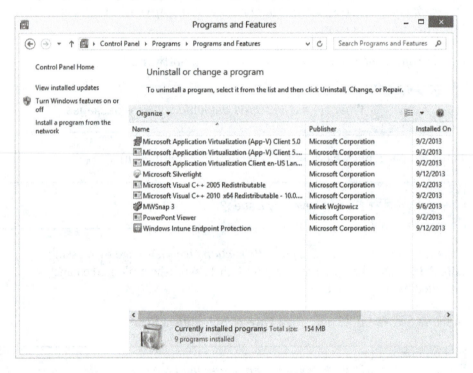

Figure 12-3
Uninstalling or changing a program

3. Click **Windows Intune Endpoint Protection** and then click **Uninstall**. Click **Yes** to uninstall the program.

4. On the *Windows Intune Endpoint Protection Uninstall Wizard* page, click **Uninstall**.

5. When the wizard is finished, take a screen shot of the *Completing the Windows Intune Endpoint Protection Uninstall Wizard* page by pressing **Alt+Prt Scr** and then paste it into your Lab 12 worksheet file in the page provided by pressing **Ctrl+V**.

Question 10	What does the note state about the protection of Windows?

6. Click **Finish**.

7. Close the **Control Panel**.

End of exercise. Leave the *Windows Intune* page open for the Lab Challenge.

Lab Challenge	Customizing the Windows Intune Company Portal
Overview	To complete this challenge, you must demonstrate how to customize the Intune Company Portal.
Mindset	You are an administrator for the Contoso Corporation. You want to customize the Company Portal so that users know where to get help with computer-related issues. Specify the steps necessary to configure the Company Portal so that a support website URL will be displayed.
Completion time	10 minutes

Write out the steps you performed to complete the challenge. When you have configured the Company Portal to display a support website URL, take a screen shot of the Company Portal page and paste it into your Lab 12 worksheet file.

End of lab.